FOULDEN, BERWICKSHIRE : J CAMPBELL KERR

COMMON LANE

Along this very lane, they say,
Roman soldiers made their way,
And Vikings, seeking worlds to pillage,
Rested here, close by the village,
And Saxon serfs and Norman lords
Crossed the river
In their hordes,
Then Cavaliers and Roundheads came
And highwaymen of dubious fame.
But all of that was long ago,
It does not touch the world we know.
Now through the bracken and the grass
Rabbits, foxes, badgers pass,
Families on nature rambles,
And children come to pick the brambles.

— Jean Harris.

People's Friend Annual 1993

CONTENTS

BACK COVER Aysgarth Falls, River Ure, Wensleydale.
Photographs on pages 25, 64, 73, 88, 123, and 140 by the
National Trust For Scotland.
Photograph on page 148 by the National Trust.

THE party was in full swing, the party Keith had looked forward to for ages. He'd wondered if he should ask Gemma to come with him, but Tracey was on night-duty at the hospital and it was impossible for her to change shifts.

Gemma was prettier by far than Tracey. She had all the glamour of her dancing profession, perfect eyes, perfect teeth, perfect hair, perfect figure.

He'd hesitated about asking Gemma to come with him to his sister Jean's celebration of her 10th wedding anniversary because Gemma was an only child, unused to large families, and Keith's was fairly large.

Gemma, possibly quite unconsciously like many people in entertainment, liked to be centre stage even when she wasn't working! She'd not have much chance of that amid the bustle and clamour

by JO COATSWORTH

6

of five brothers and sisters having a get-together, accompanied by wives, husbands and respective children, to say nothing of other relatives and friends.

The laughter, squabbling, teasing, coming and going were what Keith welcomed after the solitary indifference of life in the city. He enjoyed, however briefly, being part of the family again. Strangely, it had never occurred to him to wonder if Tracey would fit in, probably because he always envisaged nurses as able to cope with everyone and everything.

KEITH took Gemma a glass of wine. She was talking to Kirsty, Jean's eldest daughter.

"How did you hurt your leg, Gemma?" Kirsty was asking.

"Nothing very dramatic, I'm afraid." Gemma laughed. "I was late for rehearsal and hurrying to get on stage. Somehow I slipped and broke my leg."

"On stage?" Kirsty's eyes were round. "Are you an actress?"

"A dancer."

"I want to be a dancer when I grow up!"

"I hope you succeed, but I hope you have more luck than I've had."

Oh, dear, Keith thought, here we go again.

"What do you mean, Gemma?"

"The show was going to Broadway, but obviously I couldn't go with it, with a broken leg."

Gemma sighed, and Kirsty's eyes were blue pools of sympathy.

"Don't be upset, Kirsty." Gemma smiled bravely. "I could have broken my back, and then I'd never have danced again. As it is, I've just missed a wonderful opportunity."

Kirsty snuggled up to Gemma.

"Will you be able to go another time?"

"Who knows, Kirsty, who knows? I'd like to think so." Gemma's voice was wistful.

A DAY TO REMEMBER

"Still," Kirsty said brightly, "if you'd gone to America you couldn't be here with us now, could you?"

Gemma could do nothing else but agree.

"Kirsty, when's your Great Aunt Emma coming?" Keith asked.

"Mummy said she wasn't coming."

"Aunt Emma not coming? Why ever not?"

"Mummy said she wasn't very well."

"Who's Aunt Emma?" Gemma asked. "Is she someone special?"

"She is to us. Aunt Emma is — or was when we were young — almost like a fairy godmother. She always knew when things were rough and we really needed a special treat, but there was nothing sentimental about her. We seldom got any sympathy, she was always very matter-of-fact."

He was about to say more about Aunt Emma, but hesitated. Would the only child of well-off parents really understand how precious Aunt Emma's treats had been to a family like theirs?

He remembered his mother saying proudly, "I'm not poor, I'm rich in family."

And so they had been. The bond between mother and children, between brothers and sisters, had been forged to some extent from necessity. Their lack of material resources meant they had to rely on each other for amusement, help and support, but what had bound them together most of all, was their fear of their father. His drinking had made it a never-ending battle to make ends meet, his violence and bad temper had overshadowed their young lives.

Keith had hesitated too long. Now Gemma was in conversation with one of his cousins.

"Excuse me a moment, Gemma," Keith interrupted, "I must find Jean and see why Aunt Emma isn't here. I'll be back in a minute."

He found Jean in the kitchen, putting another batch of sausage rolls in the oven to be warmed.

JEAN," he said, "where's Aunt Emma?"

"She wouldn't come," Jean said. "I tried to persuade her, but you know how independent she's always been. She hates the wheelchair, and I think she's afraid people might feel sorry for her. She said the wheelchair would get in the way, take up too much room."

"Wheelchair? I don't understand. Why's Aunt Emma using a wheelchair?"

"*Keith! I told you!* I 'phoned specially to let you know how poorly she was, how she couldn't do anything in the garden now, and was finding it harder and harder to manage on her own. She sold her house and went into a nursing home."

"Jean!" Keith gazed at his sister appalled. "It was a terrible line that night, I couldn't catch all you said. I just thought Aunt Emma was finding the big garden too much for her and moving somewhere smaller. I didn't realise she was ill. What's wrong?"

"I can't remember the doctor's name for it — ataxia something or other, I think. It's a muscle-wasting disease."

"She's sold her house?" Keith remembered with pleasure the terrace house with its huge rooms, the enormous back garden in which they'd had picnics, played hide and seek, climbed the trees. The garden had been their certain refuge when their father was in one of his many frightening rages. "Then she must be very ill indeed."

"Yes," Jean agreed quietly, her eyes suddenly very bright, "very ill indeed."

"Oh, Lord," Keith groaned, "and I haven't even been in touch. Whatever will she think?"

"Knowing Aunt Emma, I don't think she'll think anything! She knows you're the world's worst letter writer!"

"I must go and see her," Keith said. "I'll go tomorrow, no matter what. I'll take her somewhere nice. I'm not bothered whether or not she's in a wheelchair!"

"What about Gemma?" Jean asked. "Shouldn't you be taking her out tomorrow?"

Keith looked across the room. Gemma caught his eye and waved. With amusement Keith noticed she was smiling and animated now, obviously enjoying the attention she was receiving from the people around her. Without surprise Keith noted how many of them were male!

"I don't think Gemma will mind," Keith said, trying to sound convincing, "if I find something we can all do."

He suggested later to Gemma that next day the three of them should visit the local Waterfowl Park.

"I know you'll like it, Gemma," he said. "Lots of the ducks and geese are so tame they'll feed from your hand. There are some flamingoes too, a super woodland section and a lovely restaurant and gift shop."

"You won't be able to help me around if you're pushing your Aunt Emma in her wheelchair," Gemma pointed out.

Keith was disappointed. He had hoped Gemma would be full of enthusiasm once she'd realised how much Aunt Emma meant to them. Guiltily he found himself thinking that Tracey would have been all in favour of taking Aunt Emma out.

He wasn't being fair. It had been a long journey, and Gemma had had not only her broken leg to cope with, but also the strain of meeting so many members of his family in a very short space of time. No wonder she needed time to sleep and pull herself together.

A UNT Emma was ready when they arrived. She was as smartly dressed as ever, her blue eyes as bright and challenging as in her younger days, defying them to show any pity, but she seemed to have shrunk and twisted, and her long hair, which she used to wear in an elegant French pleat, had been cut very short.

"I like the new hair style," he said as he bent to kiss her.

"It's easier to keep tidy this way," she explained. "How are you,

Keith? You look well."

"All the better for seeing you. This is Gemma, a friend of mine. Our services are yours to command today. You'll be chauffeured wherever you fancy going, but I thought you might like to go and feed the ducks first, then have lunch at the Waterfowl Park?"

Her eyes lit up.

"I'd love to! Do you remember the first time we went? He got such a shock, Gemma, when a big goose came rushing over to be fed, that he dropped the bag of corn and ran away."

During lunch Keith sensed Aunt Emma's frustration at being unable to hold her cup, and having to be helped with her food, but she didn't complain.

He didn't expect her to ask to go to Marks & Spencer after lunch, but she did. Gemma decided to stay in the car whilst they looked round.

"I can go to Marks & Sparks any time," she pointed out.

Keith privately thought it might have been more fun for Aunt Emma if she'd had a female companion with whom to share the now rare opportunity to look around a variety of departments and see the latest furnishings and fashions.

"Where to next?" he asked. "I thought, because you probably miss your garden, you might like to go to a garden centre and see and smell some nice flowers?"

"You're a very thoughtful boy, Keith," Aunt Emma said. "That's exactly what I would like, though I hadn't realised it until you mentioned it."

"I'm not really interested in gardening," Gemma said when they arrived. "If you don't mind I think I'll just go to the coffee shop and wait for you there."

"Are you sure you don't mind?" Aunt Emma asked. "I'm being very selfish, I know, but I promise we won't be long."

They could have spent a great deal of time at the garden centre, but, knowing Gemma was sitting on her own, looked as quickly as they could at the flowers under glass, the fruit trees, roses, shrubs. They went to see the tropical and coldwater fish, then wandered through the water gardens with their water bells and fountains, before returning to the coffee shop for tea and cake.

"I saw you looking at the azaleas, Aunt Emma," Keith said. "Would you like a miniature to take back to your room?"

"I was just thinking how nice standard azaleas would look in the park I can see from my bedroom window. They're converting it to a Japanese-type garden, complete with little bridges and pagodas. I've enjoyed watching it take shape. It's almost like having a garden of my own again, with none of the work."

"We could always get a couple and I could plant them in the park where you could see them!" Keith suggested.

"What nonsense!" Aunt Emma retorted. "You've already bought us both a couple of ivies, anyway."

"Yes, for inside, not outside. I think it's a splendid idea. You'll be

REMINISCENCE

Young and agile — she was once,
Beautiful — she was once,
Slim or tall,
Plump or small,
All were once.

Babies, toddlers — all were once,
School children — all were once,
Then teenage,
Middle-age,
All were once.

Older, wiser — we are now,
Contented, peaceful — we are now,
Lost times sadden,
But memories gladden,
How we are now.
                    — Chrissie Greenslade.

the only one who knows how those azaleas got there. All the gardeners will think someone else in the hierarchy is responsible!"

"You can't possibly be serious, Keith!" Gemma said coldly.

"I absolutely forbid it!" Aunt Emma declared. "Gemma's quite right, it's a ridiculous idea." But her dancing eyes gave her away.

Gemma refused to have anything to do with the purchase of the shrubs, neither would she get out of the car when they went into the park.

They chose the position very carefully.

"Right," Keith said. "That should do it. Next spring you'll have pretty pink and apricot blossom to look down upon."

When he'd taken her back to her room, he put the ivies on her window-sill and looked out. Yes, they had chosen exactly the right spot. Aunt Emma would have a wonderful view of them, if they weren't dug out!

He glanced around the room. On the bedside table, just as it had done in her home, stood a framed photograph, a photograph of a dark-haired, younger Aunt Emma, elegant as always, surrounded by five, well-scrubbed youngsters in their shabby but clean Sunday best — Keith and his brothers and sisters.

"You've still got it," he said smiling.

"Oh, yes," Aunt Emma said firmly. "That'll stay with me till the end."

11

Awkwardly, Keith asked, "Do you know how long, Aunt Emma?"

"No, not exactly, but not just yet."

Shocked, Keith turned away.

"Now, don't get maudlin, Keith," she said in her matter-of-fact way. "You know I hate fuss. We all go sooner or later, and I've been very lucky."

"Lucky?"

"Yes. I sometimes wondered, you know, whether it was better to have a useless mind in a healthy body, or a sound mind in a worn-out frame."

"And now you know?"

"Oh, yes, Keith, now I know. Some of the poor souls in here don't know who or where they are, or who is visiting them, *if* they get any visitors. They're lost in lonely little worlds of their own, out of touch with reality and each other. They're so solitary my heart aches for them.

"But I have memories, Keith, lots of them, and I can bring them to mind whenever I want or need them. I wasn't lucky enough to fall in love and get married, but I was blessed with five wonderful nephews and nieces who enriched my life, and I think I've been very fortunate."

"I don't know what to say, Aunt Emma."

Keith tried to control his voice.

"Don't say anything, Keith," she said, rather less briskly. "Actions speak much louder than words. I've had a wonderful time today."

"We'll have another day out," he promised, "the next time I'm up."

A S he made his way back to Gemma waiting in the car, Keith remembered the unaccustomed gentleness in Aunt Emma's voice when she said, "I've had a wonderful time today." It would, he reflected ruefully, have been even more wonderful if Gemma had shown some warmth and enthusiasm. Tracey certainly would have done so.

He'd done it again. How many times on this visit had he found himself comparing Gemma and Tracey! Why? He was under no illusion as to their different characters! In their individual ways he found them both attractive and interesting. Tracey was an uncomplicated friend, capable, understanding, reliable. As well as usually being fun to be with, Gemma was glamorous, exciting, unpredictable, and pleasure-loving. He'd always accepted that.

"What shall we do now?" she asked as he settled behind the driving wheel. "Shall we go for a drink somewhere, then out for a meal?"

Keith's mind was still on Aunt Emma, always so independent in the past, becoming increasingly helpless but without any loss of dignity or humour.

"No," he said. "I'm not really interested in doing anything like that, we can do that any time. I think we should stay in and enjoy another night with the family. Goodness knows when there'll be another opportunity for us all to meet again."

He knew quiet nights at home didn't hold much appeal for Gemma, but felt he couldn't face an evening of idle entertainment. He had a heightened awareness that life was fragile and uncertain. He wanted to enjoy tonight, treasure the memory of being together with his brothers and sisters, nephews and nieces, in case fate suddenly stepped in with an unkind hand to take away one of their number. They were obviously going to lose Aunt Emma in the not-too-distant future. He really must make the effort to come back as quickly as he could and take her out again as he'd promised.

★　　★　　★　　★

Keith was unable to keep his promise. Although he made several more visits to Aunt Emma, she was never again well enough to go out for any length of time.

Eighteen months later, with his brothers and sisters and their families, he went to the crematorium to pay his final respects to Aunt Emma.

Tracey accompanied Keith.

"Tell me about your Aunt Emma," she'd said when Keith told her his aunt had died.

"I wouldn't know where to start," Keith said. "It sounds fanciful, I know, but Aunt Emma was like a fairy godmother to us."

"With a magic wand?" Tracey teased gently.

"Oh, yes," Keith agreed. "Not that she turned pumpkins into coaches, but she always managed to 'find' bargain bits and pieces of clothing that 'might perhaps fit' when Mum hadn't much money to spare and we were all growing like weeds."

"And they always did, of course?"

"Invariably. She loved her garden, and spent a lot of time in it. So did we. We knew we were safe there."

It was in Aunt Emma's garden they'd learned about ladybirds and greenfly, seen their first bird and wasp nests, watched the "flutter-flies," picked raspberries and apples.

Keith smiled, thinking back to how they'd all had their own little plots where they could grow anything they liked. He remembered himself as a scruffy young boy proudly picking his first bag of pea-pods to take home to his mother.

"When I look back, Tracey," he said, laughing, "I realise people must have wondered what such a smartly dressed woman was doing with five shabby youngsters in tow. I remember once we went to a new Ice-Cream Parlour. It was very select, and we were very impressed. Aunt Emma bought us all the biggest ice creams there were, and then watched us with such eagle eyes in case we made a mess. We were almost too scared to eat them. Almost, but not quite!"

He seemed to talk for a long time, and Tracey listened quietly, without interruption.

"Sorry," he said at last, "I got carried away . . ."

"She was obviously very important to you," Tracey said gently, "and if she was important to you, she's important to me. I'd like to go to the funeral with you, if I may."

"Don't feel you have to come," he'd said, but she'd insisted, and he'd been glad. Gemma was on tour, but even if she'd been home, Keith knew she wouldn't have wanted to go with him.

On a beautiful spring day they said their final goodbye to Aunt Emma.

Once the service and formalities were over, Keith excused himself. "I'm not coming straight back to the house," he said to Jean. "There's something I'd like to do first, but it won't take long."

He drove to the Nursing Home and asked if he could see the Matron.

"I'd like to spend a moment or two in my aunt's room, if I may."

The matron took them in.

"She went the way I think she wanted to go," she told them. "Quietly, on her own, and with dignity. When I looked in on her shortly after breakfast, she was in her chair beside the window. She was smiling, and looked very happy and peaceful."

"Smiling?" Keith queried.

"Of course she was smiling," Tracey said who'd gone ahead to the window. "She was a very contented lady. She knew how much she was loved. The living proof of that was there before her."

Tears were in her eyes as she moved aside to let Keith see for himself. In the Japanese garden in the park opposite was a glorious froth of apricot and pink blossom.

They looked at it quietly for a few moments, then Tracey gently touched Keith's arm.

"Come along, Keith," she said. "Jean will be wondering where we are and we've got another call to make yet."

"Oh? Where?"

"The garden centre you told me about. I don't think your Aunt Emma would like it if we took her azaleas out of the park, but I think it would be nice if you bought two more and started another Japanese-type garden, to commemorate a very special lady."

Their eyes met, and Keith saw the sympathy and understanding in Tracey's. That look seemed to release something inside Keith. Not something new, but something quiet, deep and wonderful that must have been growing for quite some time. Something to which Gemma's glamour and glitter had blinded him, but which he now recognised.

Keith held out his hand, and Tracey slipped hers inside it.

"Aunt Emma's not the only special lady I know," he said. "It's a pity you didn't meet her, Tracey. She'd have liked you. She'd have liked you a lot! Well, what are we waiting for? Let's go and do something about a Japanese Garden of our own."

Still hand in hand they made their way towards the car, then set off on the road to the garden centre. □

I T'LL only be temporary, Jenny." Greg Cameron looked down at his sister with the smile for which he was well known.

Its charm had little effect on Jenny, who regarded his six-foot frame with dismay.

"Only temporary" could have been described as the theme of Greg's life — temporary jobs, temporary girlfriends, temporary enthusiasms and temporary borrowings from his sister.

Piggy-In-The-Middle

by
MARGARET BLACK

She tried to stiffen herself against the pleading in his spaniel-brown eyes, so like her own, determined that this time things would be different. She rocked back on her heels, with which she always hoped to disguise her lack of inches, and shook her head at Greg.

By working hard and saving hard, by pruning her social life to the minimum and economising on holidays, she had managed at last to move from her cramped, old flat to this one, which contained the dream of her life — an extra bedroom. No longer would her guests, or more often herself, have to sleep on a shake-down on the living-room floor.

The extra bedroom was no more than a slice of space, with a skylight window, just enough room to squeeze a single bed behind the door, three pegs on the wall to use for a wardrobe, a small chest with three drawers and one chair.

But it was still a spare bedroom. She could invite her friends to stay in comfort.

Now her brother, between jobs as ever, wanted to move in and the very idea made her grit her teeth.

"Only temporary, Jenny," he pleaded again. "Just till I have time to get myself fixed up."

"But I've invited Louise to come for the holiday weekend — "

"I'll be gone long before that! It's three weeks yet and I've got these interviews lined up — "

JENNY went on protesting weakly, but she could hear her voice growing more and more uncertain. She could no more stand out against Greg now than when he was five years old to her six and had demanded first choice of her birthday chocolates.

"Oh, all right," she said finally. "But remember Louise is coming. It's only — "

"Temporary!" A broad grin spread over his face. "I promise."

Greg moved in that night and at once all pretence at tidiness flew out of the window. With difficulty, the extra bedroom held him and some of his belongings. It did not hold his music centre, his guitar, his cassettes or his paperbacks.

Jenny told him to make use of half of her own wardrobe, then stacked every available ledge and flat surface with his cassettes, records and books. She hoped for the best — but it did not come.

Instead, Ralph Petrie arrived, breathing disapproval through his finely-cut nostrils. He also disapproved of Jenny taking on the bigger flat. What was the sense, he said, when they were going to get married?

He was very sure of that and sometimes Jenny was, too, but not quite all of the time. She could not help thinking life would be easier if Ralph and Greg got on better, instead of sniffing around each other like two wary dogs.

Ralph had a car, a flat and an excellent job in accountancy. Ralph was responsible, had smoothly-brushed, fair hair and his tie was always neatly knotted. Greg rarely wore a tie at all.

In only one way were the two young men at one. They heartily disapproved of each other.

"Couldn't you find anyone better for yourself than that lump of dough?"

"You ought to be firmer with that brother of yours, Jenny. He has no sense of responsibility at all!"

Jenny felt more and more like a bone between two unfriendly dogs.

"It's only temporary," she excused Greg.

Ralph narrowed his blue eyes. "I'll believe that when it happens! You let him walk all over you."

He stabbed the air with his forefinger. "Once we're married there'll be no more of it. I'm telling you that now!"

Jenny stiffened. No matter how much truth there was in what Ralph said, she did not like him criticising her brother.

"If you don't take a firm stand with him, he'll be here for ever!"

Jenny had an uncomfortable feeling that Ralph might be right, although she would never admit it.

When Greg moved in and day began to follow day, Jenny found her patience was becoming strained to the limit. Greg's unending supply of coffee mugs left wet circles on the furniture, he left his clothes lying all over the place, and the flat always smelled of either Indian or Chinese carry-outs. His pop music blasted her eardrums, and the nice old lady who lived next door complained about the noise.

Greg was contrite, bought a bunch of violets for the old lady, and came back from making his apologies carrying a plate of newly-baked pancakes.

"He could talk himself into the kindom of heaven, that brother of yours!" Ralph declared, when Jenny told him.

"He has toned down the sound, though." Jenny was wishing now that she hadn't brought up the subject.

"Much need," Ralph growled.

THEY were having one of their infrequent meals out in a restaurant, but Jenny was merely toying with her lasagne, looking rather unhappily into the good-looking face opposite and wondering why it was that she could never agree wholeheartedly with Ralph about Greg.

Perhaps it was because Greg was the only family she had. It was different for Ralph, whose family circle was still unbroken. She couldn't expect him to understand.

"Greg's younger than I am. I feel responsible." She was trying to explain something which was difficult to put into words.

"He's hardly a child, Jenny. He's twenty-two!"

That was true, too, but Jenny pushed aside her plate, having lost all her appetite.

When, a few minutes later, Ralph referred to her brother as a lazy layabout, she did not like to hear it and said so.

It led to a coolness between her and Ralph, which had not cleared up by the time they were climbing the stairs to the flat.

"Come in for a coffee." Jenny was beginning to feel guilty, because it seemed that she and Ralph were disagreeing so often these days.

Greg was in — and he was not alone. A red-haired young man was standing rather helplessly in the middle of the living-room floor, while Greg rolled out a sleeping-bag.

"Plenty of room for you here, Malcolm," he was saying enthusiastically. "Just stick your things behind the sofa.

"Oh, here's my sister! Jenny, this is Malcolm Wilson. He's got a burst pipe in his flat and he's flooded out. I said it would be all right for him to sleep here for a couple of nights till his place dries out."

Behind her, Jenny heard Ralph snort.

"It's only temporary," Greg said cheerfully.

It was the familiar phrase and its effect on Jenny was electric.

"It had better be!" she ground out in an icy voice.

She stalked across the floor and into her own bedroom, slamming the door after her with such force that the pictures on the wall shook.

From behind the closed door, she heard angry voices, with Ralph's incisive tones cutting through the lower-pitched rumble of Greg's words.

She looked round her bedroom and saw the wardrobe door hanging half-open and Greg's jacket trailing on the floor out of it. That seemed like the last straw.

Tears filled her eyes and she brushed them aside angrily, but she couldn't stop them. Dabbing at them fiercely with the corner of the sheet, she told herself this was the time for action.

But it was five minutes later before she was able to straighten her shoulders, blow her nose and open the door.

A S usual, Ralph and her brother were glaring at each other, this time over the head of the red-haired Malcolm Wilson, who was on his knees rolling up the sleeping-bag.

As she watched, he heaved himself to his feet.

"I," he said, with a surprising cold authority, which cut through the noisy exchange, "am leaving, so there is no need for either of you to say another word.

"You, Greg, are a bonehead not to have told me your sister's flat was so small. When you said she had an extra bedroom, I thought you meant there was room in it for both of us.

"And you," he looked at Ralph, "are going on at Greg as if you owned the place. Do you?"

Ralph's face grew scarlet. His blue eyes narrowed, as they always did when he was angry.

"No, I don't," he snapped.

"That's right." Greg nodded. "You don't. It's my sister's flat and I can invite who I like into it. Don't go, Malcolm. Jenny'll calm down."

He was still protesting as he escorted Malcolm Wilson out of the house and downstairs with his belongings.

Ralph became aware of Jenny standing silently in the open bedroom door.

"At least we've got rid of him!" he said with obvious satisfaction. "As for that brother of yours, Jenny, words fail me — "

Jenny wished they did. She looked across at the successful, good-looking young man who wanted her to marry him, and knew, in a blinding flash of self-knowledge, that she never could.

She simply couldn't look forward to a life with Ralph, when he didn't like Greg — and that meant she didn't really love Ralph, or it wouldn't have mattered whether he criticised her brother or not.

She pleaded a headache and Ralph left without coffee, distinctly huffed. It had been the opposite of a successful evening, and Jenny was thankful to be left alone, sitting down in the nearest armchair and resting her aching head against a cushion.

WHEN Greg arrived back an hour later, his face was lit up with its usual smile.

"Malcolm's got a place for a couple of nights, and, when he moves back into his own flat, I'm going with him. It'll be only temporary, of course, till I can afford a place of my own."

"Of course." Jenny stirred her own coffee and filled a mug for her brother.

"I asked Malcolm to come back with me for a coffee after he was fixed up — said you didn't make a habit of slamming doors on my friends — but he wouldn't and told me I was a bonehead to suggest it.

"He'll come tomorrow, if it's all right with you. You don't mind, do you, Jen?"

Jenny leaned her chin on her hand and said she didn't mind at all. She didn't mind that Malcolm Wilson had called her brother a bonehead more than once, either.

That was surprising, but other things were surprising, too. She should be miserable after such an evening — and she wasn't.

She should be ashamed of losing her temper and being so inhospitable to Greg's friend — and she wasn't.

She should be deeply unhappy, because now she knew there was no future for herself and Ralph. Instead of that, she was relieved.

"Are you serious about that Ralph character?" Greg demanded suddenly.

Jenny was startled and felt colour rising in her cheeks. She thought about Ralph with his quick judgments of everyone and his ready criticism.

Then, unbidden, came the memory of a shock of red hair above a pleasant, ordinary face.

"Not really," she admitted and avoided her brother's gaze. "It was — only temporary." □

Farmer's Girl

by MARY GORST

IT was the third week in July 1938, very hot with thunder in the air. The time was about 8 p.m., and I was swinging our old butter-churn round and round. Perspiration was running not only down my face but down my body as well.

I think the thunder in the air had something to do with the cream not turning into butter.

I resolved there and then, on that July night in 1938, that I would never, ever marry a farmer. I was sick of farming. I was the only daughter, in fact, the only offspring of John and Anne Gardner on their fell farm, near Abbeystead.

By nine o'clock my cream turned into butter. I took the butter out of the churn and left it on a stone slab whilst I rinsed out the churn.

I patted the butter into pound sizes, then wrapped them in grease-proof paper.

After making 12 pounds of butter, I prepared my baskets for market the next day. I wrapped four fowls which I had plucked earlier in the day and placed them in my basket. To this I added the three rabbits which Dad had caught and I had skinned, as well as four dozen eggs and the butter.

It was near twelve o'clock when I went up to bed under the rafters, halfway up the stairs.

I sat Lancaster market every Friday — in other words, I took one of the benches to sell my farm produce — and I had to be up at 5.30 a.m.

AT 6.30 a.m. next morning, I set off with my load down the road to Lancaster, over the moor, past Jubilee Tower to Quernmore. From Jubilee Tower, on a clear day, you could see Blackpool Tower, the Ribble estuary and the boats going out of Heysham to the Isle of Man.

I often drew up Prince just after the Tower and would gaze across, wondering what the world was like outside the confines of our small Wyre Valley. Where were those ships going to? What would it be like to spend a week's holiday in Blackpool?

I suppose you had to have money to go for a holiday in Blackpool. I was 18 and had never been on a holiday.

I hadn't any money. Why? Well, I was the only child on our farm and I wasn't allowed to go out either to work in a town, or in service. Father said, and his word was law, that a daughter should stay at home, where her place was.

In other words, as he hadn't a son to help him on

the farm, I was to be the son, but in addition, I was to help Mother in the house. Pay — not a penny. If I complained Mother would give me 10 shillings, and on rare occasions, if I needed a pair of shoes, she would give me £1.

When I mentioned about being paid for my labour, Mum always said, "You'll get all we have when we die."

Well, Dad wasn't a very hard worker and Mother's family weren't known for exerting themselves, either. I couldn't see that there would be much money, and as they were only tenants and not owners, all the money we had was represented by the cows and sheep.

My parents didn't believe in banks. Mother kept any money from sales of livestock in a tin on the mantelpiece above the kitchen stove.

I knew this because one day I had taken the tin down and it contained £580. In 1938, £580 was a fair amount of money, but not enough to set me up on my own farm.

Well, on that Friday in the third week of July 1938, I was up just after 5 a.m., fed my calves then lit the fire.

In those days if you wanted to boil a kettle, you lit the fire in the hearth and waited for the kettle on the spit to boil. Unless you had done so the night before, you had to go out to the pump in the yard and prime it till it gave you water from the bottom of the well.

When the kettle boiled, I made a pot of tea and took a mug up to Mum.

I had my porridge and a bacon sandwich.

"I'm off!" I shouted up the stairs.

I put my baskets in the back of the float. Prince and I jogged down to Abbeystead Bottom, then I got out and walked up out of the valley bottom to about a mile before Jubilee Tower. It was a hard pull for any horse.

I reached Lancaster about 8.30 a.m., and stabled Prince and the trap at the Fenton Street stables.

I wished I had been able to take Prince to the top of the market and leave him there while I took my two heavy baskets to my bench, but in those days there were trams in Lancaster, single-deckers known as coffin trams. If one had come clanging along, Prince would have bolted.

I slung the baskets over my arms and went to my stall in the market. I will always remember that third week in July 1938 as I struggled from the stables to the market stall, wondering if it was all worth it.

I was really depressed as I laid out my wares.

"Hello, Mary."

I looked up and there was Janet. She had been in the same class as I was at school, but she had left home to take up a job in a solicitor's office in Lancaster.

I sat there in a skirt and jumper made by my mother, as though I had come from the wilds. Janet was in a yellow and black spotted, sleeveless dress, high heels and carrying a shoulder bag. It was obvious by her hands that she had never fed calves, milked a cow or done any work on a farm.

She chatted pleasantly enough, but I felt a real country bumpkin.

As Prince and I went home later, I brooded — I think that's the right word — about my life, or lack of life and money.

As I lay on my iron bedstead that night and looked out of my lattice window, I cried to myself. If only I could get away from home and earn a few pounds, I would feel more independent.

T HE following Friday, after Janet had stopped and spoken to me, I noticed that Miss Entwhistle hadn't called and taken her usual chicken, butter and eggs. In fact, it struck me she hadn't been to see me for two Fridays.

She was one of my regular customers, a real lady. You could tell by the way she dressed and spoke.

I knew she lived in a big house at Haverbricks. It was an area where — so I thought — all the moneyed people of Lancaster lived.

I liked Miss Entwhistle, so when I went back to the stables and harnessed Prince, I thought I would go and visit her.

Looking back, here was I, a farmer's daughter who sat the market, having the audacity to visit Miss Entwhistle in her big house.

Prince and I trotted up the long drive. I had second thoughts when I saw the steps leading up to the front door.

"Hello! How nice to see you!"

I hadn't noticed Miss Entwhistle as she tended a flower bed.

I'll always remember her coming over to the trap. She was smiling, a smile I'll never forget.

I don't know why, but I said, "I'm pleased to see you. I thought you might be ill."

"Mary, how kind of you to come. Tom!" she called out.

Tom, the gardener, appeared.

"Look after Miss Gardner's horse for a while."

I was given no option but to come in for tea. She pulled a cord by the fireplace and a maid appeared.

"Tea for two, please."

We chatted, and she asked me about the farm and my place on it.

The door swung open.

"Oh, Sis! Sorry, I didn't know you had a guest."

"Come in. Miss Gardner, this is my young brother."

"Less of the young — you'd think I was still at school."

"Aren't you?"

I learned he wasn't at school but studying to be a vet at Edinburgh University.

"What's that you've brought?" Miss Entwhistle asked.

"It's a pigeon. Ma Poss refuses to pluck any more. Will you do it?"

I learned that Ma Poss was Mrs Postlethwaite, the cook. They were plagued with pigeons in their vegetable garden and Harry, Miss Entwhistle's young brother, had been thinning them out with his gun.

There was a knock on the door and the maid entered with the tea.

"Please bring another cup, Alice, and take that poor bird and put it on a cold slab. I suppose you'll have tea with us, Harry?"

"Of course — it's not often I get female company other than yourself."

It was interesting to hear the banter between brother and sister, who obviously thought the world of one another.

During tea, I learned that Miss Entwhistle's first name was Esther.

"Miss Gardner, can you pluck a pigeon?"

"Harry, you can't ask Miss Gardner to pluck them," his sister protested.

"Well, there isn't any harm in asking, is there?"

I liked Master Harry, as he was called in the household, so I answered by saying, "I can pluck pigeons, but I'll teach you how and you won't have to rely on Ma Poss."

"Harry, you've met your match!" Esther declared.

I learned later that Harry was 18, the same age as myself, and his sister was 23. Their mother had died two years ago, and Esther had stayed at home to run the house for her father who was a very well-known and very successful lawyer in Lancaster.

HARRY jumped up and held out his hand. "Come on, give me a lesson."

Without thinking, I took his hand and was whisked down to the kitchen.

"Ma Poss, Miss Gardner is going to give me lessons in pigeon plucking."

I borrowed a carving knife from Ma Poss, as well as a pair of scissors and a ball of thin string.

We went into the outbuildings, sat on two boxes and I plucked the feathers into another. I plucked them off the breast, then handed it over to Harry to do the other breast.

He was too impatient and tore the skin, but managed to do the legs better.

"What's you first name?" Harry asked.

"Mary," I replied.

"I'm really enjoying this lesson, Mary."

I then showed him how to cut the head off, take out the innards and truss the legs.

"Come on, Mary, let's show Ma Poss what we've done."

"Not bad. Who tore it?" she asked.

"Me," Harry replied.

He grabbed a plate, placed his pigeon on it and mounted the stairs two at a time.

"Esther, where are you?"

I followed more sedately.

Esther was knitting at one of the lounge windows overlooking the garden.

She wouldn't believe that Harry had nearly done it all himself.

"Harry, you've taken up too much of Miss Gardner's time already.

She has to go back to Abbeystead, you know, next to the farm where your grandad was born. Go and fetch her trap and we'll meet you at the front door."

I was in no hurry to leave, but it would take me two hours to get home. I jumped into the trap, thanked Esther for my tea and wished Harry luck in his pigeon-plucking.

"I'll let you know how I get on, Mary. 'Bye."

" 'Bye, Miss Gardner," Esther said as Prince and I trotted down the drive.

I was over two hours later than usual. Mother was in a state.

I explained about Miss Entwhistle, but I said nothing about pigeons and Harry.

T HE following Thursday evening I was churning butter in the dairy when I heard the roar of a car as it entered our yard. I could see who was at the wheel of that long, open car — it was none other than Harry Entwhistle.

Mother went to the door. She told me afterwards that he had raised his cap and asked if I was about.

▶ *over*

Glorious Gardens

Brodick Castle, Isle of Arran

T HERE has been a castle on this commanding spot, overlooking Brodick Bay, since Viking times, but the woodland garden dates from 1923. It was established by Mary, Duchess of Montrose, and is renowned for its collection of rhododendrons — some 260 species — which thrive on the rich soils and sheltered slopes below the castle.

From April to June the grounds are ablaze with colour — a wooded wonderland between Arran's rugged mountains and the sea.

"Mary, there's a young man asking for you," she called to me from the door of the dairy.

"Ask Harry to come in here."

"Hello, Mary, I've come to show you something," he greeted me. "Come into the car."

I smiled, and he grabbed my hand, just as he had done when we went for his lesson on pigeon plucking.

He carefully unwrapped the greaseproof paper surrounding a small parcel to reveal a plucked pigeon. It was beautifully plucked, not a torn piece of skin, and the legs were tied as I had shown him.

"You've done it, Harry! It's even better than I'd have done it," I told him.

"Thanks, Mary." He put his hands on my shoulders and gave me a peck on the cheek.

I was certain that Mother was watching from the kitchen window.

"I've brought you six pigeons to sell at the market tomorrow," Harry went on.

I noticed that these six were not plucked.

"Come on, you can churn while I pluck — they won't sell unplucked," I reminded him.

John churned till his back ached, while I plucked, cleaned and dressed his six pigeons.

I then patted the butter into pounds, counted out the eggs, and put the fowls and the pigeons into greaseproof paper.

"Come and meet Mum and Dad," I invited.

They were in the kitchen, all agog to meet the young stranger.

"Mum, Dad, this is Harry Entwhistle, Miss Entwhistle's young brother."

"Don't you start, Mary — I get enough of that young stuff from our Esther," Harry said.

He shook hands with Mum and Dad.

"Harry has brought me six pigeons to sell," I explained. "He's helping me with an idea of mine."

Harry looked at me and agreed, but I knew he hadn't a clue what I was talking about.

I left him talking to Mum and Dad about farming and his grandad coming from the next farm, while I changed into a summer dress and ran a comb through my hair.

Harry took the hint when I returned downstairs, and within minutes we spun out of the yard in his car.

"Where are we going, Harry?"

"For a drink — so that I can learn about the idea I'm supposed to be helping you with."

We travelled through the twisty road of the Trough of Bowland at a steady pace, and pulled up in front of an imposing hotel. I'd passed it once or twice on the way to Clitheroe Market, but never thought I would enter its doors.

"Harry, I've never been in a hotel before. What do I drink?"

He turned in his seat and gave me a peck. "Mary, you're special.

Not many girls would have been honest and admitted they'd never had a drink before."

We went into a bar which was full of fishermen, gamekeepers and other visitors, with a big log fire burning. We found a free table, and Harry went for the drinks.

He came back with what he said was a draught pint and tall glass of bitter lemon for me. I'll never forget how attractive it looked — the glass containing the bitter lemon was full of ice and there was a piece of fresh lemon hanging over the edge.

"What do I do with the lemon, Harry?"

"Esther sucks it."

Well, if Esther sucked it, then that must be the thing to do. I did likewise — it was really sour.

"Now, Mary, what's this idea I'm supposed to be helping you with?" Harry went on.

HARRY was easy to chat to so I told him how frustrated I was. I explained about not getting wages for the work I did on the farm and how tired I was of working the long hours.

I told him that I wanted to be independent and have a business of my own. I didn't like the idea of being tied to my Mum and Dad's farm for the rest of my life.

"Harry, I haven't been taught anything. I can't type or do any office work. What should I do?"

Harry came from a family who knew how to make money. He took my hands and looked into my face.

"Mary, you can do better than type for a few shillings a week," he assured me. "You can sell goods, and you can breed stock. You've done it since you left school."

We chatted about selling more goods at my stall at the market and about how I could breed my own stock.

I noticed it was 10.30 p.m. on the clock which hung over the bar counter.

"Harry, I've got to be away by 6.30 a.m. for Lancaster for market tomorrow. We'd better get home," I said.

"What time do you have to be at the market, Mary?"

"About 8.30 a.m."

"I'll be up at Abbeystead before 8.00 a.m. to run you to Lancaster. Is that all right?"

It was the appealing way he said it that really got me. I leaned across the table, gave him a kiss, and said excitedly, "Yes, Harry, please come."

Harry dropped me off in our yard. "See you tomorrow, Mary. 'Night, dear."

When I went into the kitchen, Mum and Dad were waiting up for me.

"Where have you been?"

"I've been out with Harry for a drink."

I smiled, for I knew they were thinking I was drunk.
They went on and on at me.
"What's he helping you with?" Dad demanded.
"As you don't even give me a wage, I'm going to sell things on my own and start breeding my own stock. Good night."

★　　★　　★　　★

Dad gave me a shout at 5.30 a.m. I turned over and went to sleep. If he wanted his early morning cup of tea in bed, he could go down into our cold, flag-floored kitchen, light the fire and wait for the kettle to boil!

He came into my room and shook me. "Mary, it's market day."

"I know it is. Harry's coming to pick me up at eight o'clock to take me."

What he went back to Mother and said, I never heard, but they were, I'm sure, two worried parents. They had lost their unpaid slave.

I packed the butter, Harry's six plucked pigeons, chickens, rabbits and eggs into my baskets.

Harry drove into the yard at 7.50 a.m. You couldn't help but hear the roar of the car. I came out of the back door carrying my heavy baskets as it drew to a halt.

Harry jumped out and carried my baskets. He opened the car door and ushered me in before running around to the driver's side.

Harry drew up at Jubilee Tower and parked the car so that we could look over to Blackpool, the Ribble estuary and Morecambe.

LEISURE

I thought today would be the best,
A free day full of joy and rest,
I put my hands behind my head,
Enjoying Sunday's lie in bed.

Perhaps I'll walk down to the sea,
Sit in the garden with my tea,
A picnic, or a gentle hike,
A lazy ride upon my bike?

Which one to choose? I must decide,
I throw the curtains open wide,
I see the rain upon the pane,
And jump back into bed again.

— Chrissy Greenslade.

"Mary, why don't you buy things in bulk and sell them in pounds, like the shops do? You could fatten your own pigs and lambs, be your own boss and make money. I'll help you if you'll let me," he offered.

"I'd like that, Harry."

He gave me a kiss even although it was just after eight in the morning.

Farmer's Girl

"Come on, let's start. I've gathered ten pounds of Victoria plums for you to sell today. They're in one pound bags — ask for sixpence a bag," he instructed.

He carried my heavy baskets and his basket of plums to my table in the market. He stayed and showed me how to lay them all out to look their best.

I had never bothered to lay them out before.

Mrs Ashton, one of my regular customers, came just after nine o'clock for her butter and eggs.

"Oh, you've got pigeons. I'll take all six," she decided.

She went on to tell me that she was having six people in for dinner and would give them each a pigeon. She also bought two pounds of plums.

By noon I had sold out and could have sold lots more, thanks to the way Harry had laid out my wares.

Harry arrived just after twelve o'clock to see how I was getting on.

"Harry, I've sold out, thanks to you."

"Good, let's go for lunch."

And off we went.

HARRY took me home and explained that he had to go back for his next year to the Royal Dick Vet College in Edinburgh. He asked if he could take me out one Saturday night, when we could discuss some suggestions on how to enlarge my buying and selling and breeding business.

As we sat in a hotel that Saturday night, I learned that Harry had really been doing his homework on my behalf. He suggested two channels. First, rent a store in the market not far from my stall, buy potatoes, carrots, turnips, etc., in bulk and sell them by the pound.

Secondly, he advised me to get my own stock on the farm.

"Mary, your farm has a pigsty with no pigs," he pointed out. "Buy six and fatten them. Take grazing and put bullocks on it in summer."

I did everything he suggested, and soon began to make money.

Harry went back to college but came down south every second weekend. His sister, Esther, who became one of my best friends, said he had never done so before.

When Harry got his degree Esther, his father and I went up to see him capped in Edinburgh. Both his father and Esther were very nice to me and they paid all the hotel bills.

We celebrated his success by having a dinner at the Cramond Inn, just outside Edinburgh. I had never in my life had such an enjoyable three days.

I rented a farm on a nearby estate, and Harry joined a vet practice in Lancashire.

Yes, we did get married. I can hardly believe that next week Harry and I are going to see our son get his vet's degree. Afterwards, we shall go to the Cramond Inn for a celebration dinner.

We've come a long way since I taught Harry how to pluck a pigeon . . . ☐

JANICE cast her first spell at the local Flower Show — not that she realised she'd done so, at least not then.

She'd taken in the embroidered pictures and tapestry firescreen she was entering for the handicraft section, and was on her way out of the marquee when she bumped into Fred Greenway, the caretaker of the office block where Janice worked.

"Hello, Fred," she said. "What have you put in? I bet it's flowers. I'll never forget the wonderful gladioli you gave me when I was twenty-one!"

"Hello, Janice!" Fred smiled. "Yes, I'm trying again — not just flowers, though, vegetables, too. This'll be my last year, so I thought I'd make a

Bewitched?

special effort. I've been close several times, but I've always been pipped at the post."

"I don't understand, Fred." Janice frowned. "Why will it be your last year?"

"I'm retiring in January, and we're moving to the Midlands to be near our daughter. We've already bought a flat. Very nice it is, too, but no garden, of course, and no allotments nearby."

"Oh, Fred, I'm sorry. You'll really miss your garden, won't you?"

"Yes, but in a way it's a blessing. I've a lot of bother with my back and knees these days. Still, it would be nice to go out in a blaze of glory, wouldn't it? Tell you

what, Janice, if I win a cup I'll fill it with something nice and you can have the first sip."

"You're on!" Janice agreed. "Where are your entries, Fred? Let's go and look at them, shall we, and see how much competition you've got?"

THEY inspected the banks of glowing flowers, the prime selection of vegetables. Janice looked closely at Fred's pearly white leeks with their tasselled roots, cabbages as big as pumpkins, cucumbers like green loofahs. She couldn't help noticing Fred's eyes resting wistfully on the silver cups displayed at the bottom of the marquee.

Fred was a gentle, obliging

by RITA DAWSON

old man to whom nothing was ever too much trouble, and Janice was very fond of him. It was obvious how much he'd like to win a trophy.

I do hope he does, Janice thought, but I don't know . . . His entries are very good, but I can't tell if they're the best. She tried to encourage him and make him smile.

What made her say the next words she didn't know — she put it down to impulse.

"Your things look super to me, Fred. I'm sure you'll win this time, but just to make sure, I'll put a spell on them."

She thought of the heroine in the old TV show, "Bewitched," attempted unsuccessfully to wiggle her nose, waved her hand around in the air instead, and tried to think of a rhyme, which was much easier than she'd imagined.

"All flowers but Fred's, though now bright and gay,
Wilt and fade till Fred's win the day.
Vegetables, too, shrink and blight,
Fred's only staying a handsome sight."

They both laughed.

"What about your entries?" Fred asked. "Don't you want them to win, too?"

"One spell at a time is all I can manage," Janice joked. "Ah, well, see you on Thursday with the bubbly, Fred."

They parted, and Janice forgot about the incident until the following Thursday.

Fred came into the office mid-morning, then with a showman's flourish, produced two shining silver cups.

"Just as you said, Janice," he said, beaming. "The other things seemed to go off a bit."

He produced a fairly-large bottle of sparkly wine and poured it into the bigger of the cups. "Here you are, you little witch! I always keep my promises. I'd better, in case you put a spell on me, too!"

Fred was always generous, and he wasn't stingy with the wine. By the time the cup was empty, Janice was typing with more enthusiasm than accuracy!

"Witch," she gurgled happily a little later on as she glanced out of the window.

Ah, there you were. Every day at about that time, an old lady passed with a black Labrador dog. The dog's right foot had been bandaged for some time and it was still limping badly.

Poor thing, Janice thought sympathetically. Then she giggled.

"I'm a witch," she informed her empty office, "so I'll cast another spell."

She flapped her hands around, hiccupped, and said:

"Big black dog with poorly paw,
Within two days it'll hurt no more."

Whatever wine Fred had put into the cup had been quite potent. Even on the Friday morning Janice still had a headache, but it wasn't bad enough to stop her noticing that the dog's paw didn't seem quite so painful. On the Saturday the dog was hardly limping at all, and it was then that Janice began to wonder . . .

You're being ridiculous, she told herself, it's just coincidence. She couldn't help remembering, though, how often she'd been lucky in the past, how often she'd "wished" things would happen, and they had.

Once when she'd been at school she'd been very disappointed when she wasn't chosen to play the piano solo at the school concert. She remembered how intensely she'd wished that something would happen to the other girl! Two days before the concert she'd fallen and broken her arm, and Janice had had the solo spot after all.

It couldn't possibly have been brought about by "wishing" something would happen to the other girl! You couldn't *really* put spells on people, could you?

A shiver of apprehension, spiced with excitement, ran down Janice's spine. Well, there was one way to find out, wasn't there? She'd take on a proper challenge this time, something that would prove or disprove the idea without any doubt.

A FEW days later, the Company Secretary found he needed to go to Paris for several days on business. Unexpectedly, he decided he needed to have his secretary, Beth, go too.

There was no way, Janice mused, under normal circumstances, that she would have the opportunity to go. If Beth couldn't go for any reason, the second choice would be Vicki. Unless . . .

"Beth, I don't wish you lasting harm,
But you'll lose the use of your right arm.
Vicki, dear, by some mischance,
You won't be able to go to France."

Janice said the rhyme very firmly, and waited.

Nothing dramatic happened at first, then Beth went to the doctor's for a pre-holiday inoculation. She complained almost immediately about her arm being sore. It quickly became very swollen and inflamed, so much so that she had to go back for treatment and was given a sick note.

Vicki followed her within two days, going down with a virus infection so severe she was in bed for a week.

Janice was horrified. She hadn't really believed anything would happen!

Although she'd always wanted to go to France, Janice hated every minute she spent in Paris. She was relieved they were so busy there was no opportunity to sightsee. She felt so worried and guilty about Beth and Vicki, she wouldn't have wanted to go anyway.

Although she hadn't honestly thought she was capable of casting a spell, she should have thought more carefully before she said the rhyme, just in case. Well, she wouldn't do it again. She'd say one more, to put things right, and that would be the last.

"Beth and Vicki,
The time has come to put things right,
You'll both feel joy, have futures bright."

C

Janice was on edge for ages. She said the rhyme over and over again. It took longer than usual for this spell to work, but the results were worth waiting for.

Beth started going out with the young doctor who had had to treat her for the inoculation which had gone wrong. When they became engaged, Beth was so happy her plain face was almost beautiful.

I'm so glad, Janice thought, a lump in her throat. At least everything's worked out all right for Beth. Now, what about Vicki?

After a premium bond win, Vicki went away on a very expensive cruise, beside which Paris looked very insignificant indeed.

At last Janice was able to relax. No more spells for me, she vowed. She kept her promise, too, until Rob came on the scene.

ROB was a live-wire, brimming over with enthusiasm and new ideas. He brought fresh life and interest to the office.

As soon as Janice saw him, she knew he was special — so special she was worried her feelings would show, and kept herself aloof.

Rob was a terrible tease, and Janice was always tongue-tied when he was near, unable to think of witty responses to his joking, although the other girls had no problems. In face, she was scared to say anything in case she said something stupid or that he might not like.

She was miserable over the fact that he got on so well with the rest of the staff, but kept her distance because she feared that if she didn't, she mightn't be able to conceal how she felt about him.

FAREWELL, SUMMER

The bracken is drooping,
The martins are swooping;
The rain clouds are blackening and breaking;
The leaves are all dropping,
The pine trees need lopping,
Ripe blackberries there for the taking.

The puddles are deeper,
The anthills are steeper,
The track where we stand now is sodden;
The gorse is still yellow,
The undergrowth mellow,
But summer is almost forgotten.

— Chrissy Greenslade.

She day-dreamed a lot, imagining herself as Rob's wife, looking after him and their home, helping him with his career, looking after their three daughters. Somehow it was always three daughters, of the same age, so presumably they were triplets.

As time went on and Janice was unable to overcome her diffidence where Rob was concerned, she became very unhappy. She really tried not to, but she just couldn't help wishing Rob would notice and like her.

A verse came easily to mind, and became a thought before she could stop it:

"Rob, you may think that I don't care,
But look beneath the mask I wear,
Quite soon you're going to notice me,
And long to seek my company."

Again she waited.

One day when Janice wasn't very busy but Beth was overwhelmed with work, Janice offered to make the coffee for the Board Meeting.

She staggered down the corridor with the heavy tray, reflecting that a trolley would have made life much easier, when the world turned upside down. She fell headlong, and the flying tray shattered the glass of the fire alarm.

She lay there amid the coffee and broken crockery, too dizzy to move, her head aching, and her ears protesting at the klaxon above her head which was doing its best to deafen her and everyone else in the building.

The Board Members left the Board Room, and people spilled out of the building like water through a colander.

Rob was the one who picked Janice up and carried her outside. Fire engines arrived, very quickly, wailing like banshees.

Janice wondered what they would do when they found out that she hadn't dropped the tray because of a fright when the klaxon sounded, that it had actually been the tray that had set off the alarm!

Tearfully, she explained what had happened.

Rob went inside with the firemen, and when they came out he was furious.

"No wonder you slipped," he explained. "Workmen had spilled some oil on the floor and hadn't wiped it up properly. You're lucky you didn't break anything — apart from the cups and saucers, I mean!"

His eyes laughed into hers, but there was concern in them, too.

Janice's head ached a lot and she couldn't stop trembling. Rob took her to hospital for a check-up, then home.

Janice asked him to have a cup of coffee before he went back to work. Away from the office, she seemed to lose her inhibitions and conversation was easy. It was all plain sailing after that . . .

Later on, Janice began to worry. She wanted Rob to like her, but for herself, not because he was bewitched. Somehow it didn't seem fair to him.

It wasn't easy to tell Rob about her powers — how do you

convince someone you're a witch without them wondering about your sanity? — and promised to lift the spell.

Rob roared with laughter.

"Well," he said, "I'll admit to being enchanted from the moment we met, even though you cold-shouldered me all the time. But that was *before* you said your verse, wasn't it? So you see, you may be a little witch, but you can't work magic."

They made plans for the future. Rob said he wanted to be the Company's youngest-ever Financial Director. Janice just wanted to be a wife and mother.

"How many children shall we have?" Rob asked.

"At least four, I think. I'm sure there'll be triplets, after that I don't know."

"You're not serious?" Rob groaned. "I'll *have* to get early promotion to be able to support you all!"

THEY'D been married three years when Rob didn't get the promotion he was hoping for. They were both disappointed.

"Never mind," Janice said, "perhaps there's something better in the pipeline," and for his sake she really hoped there was.

She didn't exactly "wish," you understand, just "hoped" in a sincere, wifely kind of way that wouldn't harm anyone! She wondered why old Carstairs, who should have retired years ago, couldn't find something very interesting to do that would make him want to retire, and leave the way open for a nice promotion for someone much younger!

Quite unexpectedly, a little later, Rob was invited to a meeting at Head Office.

He swung Janice into his arms when he got home.

"You'll never guess!" he said. "Old Carstairs is getting married again! Apparently, they knew each other years ago, and have just got together again. They're both tired of being on their own. He's retiring so they can make the most of their twilight years."

"And?"

"And they've asked me to become Financial Controller of the Southern Region! I'll make Financial Director yet, just you wait and see!"

"Oh, darling, I'm so glad," Janice said. "And I'm so pleased about Mr Carstairs — that it's a nice reason he's retiring, I mean."

Rob looked keenly at her.

"Have you been casting more spells?" he asked. "I've told you before, you little goose, these things are just coincidence!"

"Of course they are," Janice agreed.

Somehow it didn't seem the right time to tell him her news. Rob knew she was pregnant, of course, but at her check-up that afternoon, although it was unknown on both sides of the family, the doctor had confirmed that there was definitely more than one baby, in fact there were probably more than two.

Janice is still not sure about being a witch . . . □

The Healing Visit

S HARNHAM AVENUE," the bus conductor
called.

Elsie Paterson sat on the bus until the other
passengers had disembarked, then slowly followed
them. She stood for a few minutes, aware of the
chatter around her, but letting it pass over her.

Then, still slowly, as though lacking motivation,
she followed the other small groups up the wide,
tree-lined avenue.

by MARY LEDGWAY

That those in front of her were regular visitors to Sharnham Hospital was obvious by the way they talked.

One elderly lady, with tears streaming down her cheeks, was comforted by her companion, a worried-looking man who looked as though he, too, needed support.

There were some in bright summer dresses, with carefully made-up faces as though determined to keep whatever grief they felt to themselves. Some people carried small bunches of flowers; others cradled huge bouquets. Smart shopping bags and plastic carriers bulged with clean clothes, towels and all the necessities of hospital life.

Elsie carried nothing. Only her shoulder-bag, blue to match her summer suit, swung against her hips. Her eyes were fixed on the hospital, standing sentinel at the top of the avenue.

It wasn't a large building, constructed in brick, which had mellowed over the years to a warm, rusty red. Originally a private house, the hospital catered mostly for maternity cases and older patients. Elsie had never visited, and even now . . .

ONCE in the grounds, Elsie sat on a seat, half-eager, half-afraid. Was Elise, her little girl, really in there? Her mind wandered back to the dreadful day when her husband, Gavin, had left home, bright and cheerful as always.

Elise had walked home up the garden path at the same time as the policeman.

A car out of control had mounted the pavement, and Gavin hadn't stood a chance. What a comfort 17-year-old Elise had been during those dreadful days.

Then, four weeks later, when Elsie was valiantly trying to put her shattered life together again, Elise had told her about the baby.

Elsie had let anger take over from grief. Elise had said little, only looked at her with wide, frightened eyes.

The next morning, after a sleepless night, Elsie had gone early to her daughter's bedroom.

"Elise, I'm sorry for some of the things I said last night, but now, I've had time to think things over. I won't deny it still hurts — but if you want to keep the baby, well, you can stay here and we'll fix something up. It isn't what I hoped for you, but we'll both just have to make the best of it.

"But you must promise not to see this — this Roger — again."

Even now, Elsie could remember the love that was in her heart, the love she couldn't express. Surely Elise would understand, she had thought.

"No, Mother! That's not what I want. I told you last night we both want this baby. We need to be together, and a baby needs two parents." Her voice broke, but she went on. "I love Roger, Mum. He's got a sort of flat, and we'll manage. Mum, please try to understand. I didn't want to hurt you, but you had to know — "

Elise had broken down in tears, but Elsie had stood up, her

daughter's tears only adding to the pain of the last few weeks.

"You've heard what I said. If you can't or won't meet me halfway, then there's no more to be said."

When she came home from work that evening, Elise had packed her belongings and gone. Elsie did telephone her office but she was not there, and when she questioned her daughter's best friend, she learned nothing.

So when asked about Elise, she simply said she had gone away for a while and was working near her aunt's in Scotland. Whether she was believed, she neither knew nor cared. She had lost her daughter as surely as she had lost her husband.

Life became a round of work, television, and sleepless nights.

Although she could control her actions, Elsie could not check her thoughts. As the weeks went by, they turned more and more to Elise.

How was she managing in her "sort" of flat? By what Elsie could remember, Roger was still serving an apprenticeship. She couldn't even recall his surname.

E LSIE'S eyes went again to the outline of the building.
It was quite by chance, at a meeting with an old friend in a café, that she had learned where her daughter was having her baby.

"I think I ought to tell you — I'm working now in the kitchens at Sharnham Hospital. Your Elise came in last night — I saw her as I was leaving. Her baby looked due any time," her friend had remarked.

Elsie couldn't glean any more, but today, three days later, she had taken her courage in both hands and come to see her daughter.

How different it had been for her when Elise was born. She remembered the love in Gavin's eyes as he held his tiny daughter.

"We'll call her Elsie."

"No, we won't." Elsie had laughed. "One Elsie in the family is enough."

"Not for me." His smile had been very tender. "Half a dozen wouldn't be too many, but I'll tell you what — how about Elise? It has the same letters, and it makes a pretty name for a pretty little girl."

How would Gavin feel if he knew she had let his beloved daughter go through the process of becoming a mother alone?

Elsie stood up, and after only the briefest pause, walked through the imposing doors.

Inside, she stood looking at the signs. A tall gentleman was in front of her. His smart grey suit contrasted sharply to most of the casual clothes of the other men, but when Elsie glimpsed his face she saw the bitter set to his mouth as he, too, walked in the direction of the Maternity arrow.

Elsie walked behind him, but when he stopped, so did she. For a moment he hesitated, then knocked on the first of the double doors marked "Nursery."

A nurse responded to his knock and had a brief consultation with him. Then she went back into the blue and white room looking at the name tabs.

When she came back, holding a small baby in her arms, Elsie watched as the man put a finger into one of the waving fists, smiling when the tiny fingers clutched his own.

Then, with one last look and a word of thanks to the nurse, he turned and walked along into the corridor.

He paused and looked in the direction of the wards, but with a barely discernible shake of his head, he turned away and walked back the way he had come.

E LSIE now followed his lead and spoke to the nurse. "Paterson, Baby Paterson."

The nurse frowned, shaking her head. "I don't think so, dear, but I'll look."

When she came back with empty arms, Elsie forced a smile. "Perhaps it hasn't arrived yet. I may have made a mistake."

Deflated, she nearly followed the unknown gentleman out of the area, but the knowledge that her daughter was here in this building stopped her.

Slowly, she walked past the ward doors. There were only four beds to a ward and suddenly, through the glass panel, she saw her.

Elsie was not prepared for the surge of emotion that flooded through her when she saw her daughter again. The baby, the quarrel, everything was forgotten as she walked up to the bed.

"Mother!" There was no mistaking the joy on Elise's face.

Suddenly their arms were round each other, their tears mingling. Then they drew apart, each looking at the loved face of the other.

"I'm sorry, Mum. It was too soon after Dad — "

Elsie hushed her. "No, love, not now. I was wrong, but we can talk later."

Suddenly she saw Elise's slim outline under the coverlet.

"Elise — the baby? There was no Baby Paterson — "

Elise's eyes were full of pride, her lips curved in a smile of pure happiness as she held out her left hand.

"Roger and I were married three weeks after I left home. I wanted you there, but — as you say, we'll talk later."

She smiled. "Now go and ask the nurse again. Baby Bentley."

Her eyes danced and Elsie recognised the old Elise.

So Elsie went again to the nursery. This time the nurse smiled, and beckoned Elsie into the nursery.

"Baby Bentley, girl, Rosemary," read the name on the cot she was led to.

Elsie held her breath as she looked at her tiny granddaughter, so perfect, so utterly wonderful.

But the nurse was beckoning her to the next cot. "Baby Bentley, boy, Gavin."

A deep gratitude filled Elsie's heart as she touched the soft, rosy cheek of the sleeping child — another Gavin. How proud her husband would have been.

She went back to the ward and sat beside her daughter. Only her eyes and the pressure of her hands told Elise how deep her mother's feelings were at that moment.

GENTLY Elise released one hand and reached inside her locker. "Take this home and read it, Mum. I was going to get Roger to post it. We both thought it was time for hard feelings to end.

"Besides, babies need a gran, and Roger hasn't any family. That's why it was so important for us to be together — "

A hint of the old anxiety clouded her eyes, but Elsie smiled. "It doesn't matter now. We'll be one big family. Elise, thank you for the letter. I'm glad you wrote."

As a pleasant nurse told her it was time to leave, she stood up, smiling a gentle farewell.

"Come tomorrow," Elise whispered. "You'll be able to nurse the babies."

Elsie nodded. If she hurried she might just catch the shops before they closed. Knitting wool, and some soft, fleecy blankets — she would not be empty-handed as she walked up Sharnham Avenue tomorrow.

At the door she saw the tall stranger. He was walking away from the wards, and he was smiling, a smile that included her as their eyes met.

"A lovely day," he remarked, and Elsie smiled back.

"A magical day," she answered, and he nodded in agreement. □

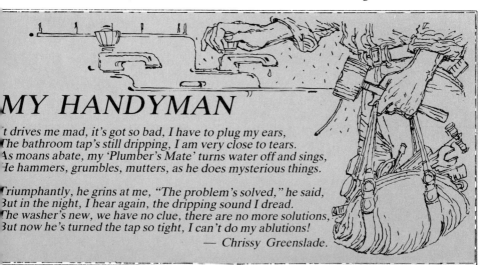

MY HANDYMAN

t drives me mad, it's got so bad, I have to plug my ears,
The bathroom tap's still dripping, I am very close to tears.
As moans abate, my 'Plumber's Mate' turns water off and sings,
He hammers, grumbles, mutters, as he does mysterious things.

Triumphantly, he grins at me, "The problem's solved," he said,
But in the night, I hear again, the dripping sound I dread.
The washer's new, we have no clue, there are no more solutions,
But now he's turned the tap so tight, I can't do my ablutions!

— *Chrissy Greenslade.*

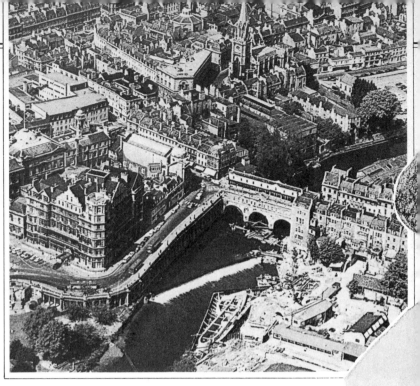

Love
Leads The Way

"ARE you the tour guide?" The American drawl held the slightest hint of mockery.

Claire's head jerked up, but as her gaze met that of the young man's, the firm denial froze on her lips.

For an instant, she detected an admiring gleam in his vivid blue eyes. then his mouth twisted into a grin.

As the fragrance of his aftershave drifted to the teenager's nostrils, her senses reeled and her mind went blank.

She was aware only that she found him most attractive . . .

Momentarily, he, too, seemed lost for words. Then, without waiting further for an answer, he extended a hand and smiled lazily

by
**JANET
BOND**

"Brad Newman."

Claire blushed at the warmth of his grip.

Suddenly she realised how he had made the mistake, for she had stopped to study her recently-purchased guide-book beside a notice pronouncing, "Guided Tours of Bath, please queue here."

She wanted to explain, that she, too, was a visitor to the city, but she was so afraid that he might just turn and walk away, the words stuck in her throat.

Instead she said simply, "Claire Taylor."

"I guess we'll be away any time now." He nodded sideways. "Quite a queue building up."

CLAIRE leaned forward to follow his gaze, her green eyes filling with panic as the group of tourists, taking their cue from the blond-haired American, surged forward, crowding round her, seemingly afraid that they were missing something.

"Shall we go, then?" Brad prompted.

His tone was slightly provocative, and Claire had the strangest feeling that he was making fun of her.

She speculated for a moment, mentally questioning her own capabilities. Surely, she reasoned, the job only called for a little commonsense.

Would it be so difficult to show this friendly-looking party around the city? Dare she?

Weighing the odds of being found out, she stole another glance at Brad's clean-cut features. What had she to lose?

Gripped by a sudden, irrational determination, her mouth quirked mischievously. Crazy though it was, she would have a go!

Claire almost laughed aloud as she remembered her horoscope in the morning paper.

"Today," it had read, "will present you with a unique challenge. Meet it with confidence and you will be well rewarded."

Hardly the sort of challenge she had envisaged, but then, thinking back, hadn't she already promised herself that today would be utterly and completely different?

Claire had woken early on the morning of her birthday with a strange tingle of excitement.

Pushing aside the bedclothes, she eased her feet to the floor, padded across to the window and pulled back the curtains.

The sun was high in an azure sky, pledging hours of warmth ahead. She made her first, uncharacteristic decision.

Wrapping her dressing-gown round her, she went downstairs to the hall telephone, and rang her office.

"I shan't be in today, Sally."

Her colleague interrupted, "Got that tummy bug that's been going around, have you?"

Claire grinned a little guiltily. "I don't think so." Inexplicably, she cared little how her words were interupted. "I just feel a little strange today, that's all."

"Happy birthday!" Having overheard Claire's telephone conversation, Mrs Taylor hurried from the kitchen to plant a kiss on her daughter's cheek.

"Not going to work today?" she chided. "That's not like you."

Claire rolled her eyes heavenward.

"Don't worry, Mum," she said. "I'm taking it as a day's holiday. I think I might go sightseeing in Bath."

After breakfast, Claire showered and dressed carefully, choosing a peach-coloured, cotton jumpsuit that flattered her slim figure and clear complexion.

"'Bye Mum," she called, moments later, from the front door.

"Be careful."

Her mother's words echoing after her, Claire set off, hair swinging, to walk to the railway station.

For her, travelling by train was unusual — she would enjoy the ride to Bath.

E AGER voices cut across Claire's memories of the morning, reminding her now of her predicament.

Unobtrusively, she tried to study the small, street map in her guide-book. Perhaps, with its help, she could bluff her way through. This was by no means her first visit to Bath, and she did have some idea of its history and landmarks.

"Follow me, please," she croaked, glancing around anxiously, fearful that at any moment the real guide would show up.

Brad grinned, and, matching his lengthy stride to her shorter one, fell into step beside her. Exchanging small talk, together they led the way through the quaint, shop-filled, flower-bedecked alleys.

Before long it dawned upon her that the tourists were growing impatient, expecting her to stop and say something of interest.

Under cover of her shoulder-bag, she sneaked another surreptitious glance at the informative book in her hand, acutely aware that a genuine guide would have no need of it.

"Bath was founded by the Romans," Claire began hesitantly.

Thirty or so eager people gathered round and someone shouted to her to speak up. Colour flooding her cheeks, she scanned them, praying that they all spoke English. Taking a deep breath, she endeavoured to project her voice.

"Because of its medicinal spring waters," she continued, "they named it, Aquae Sulis, Waters of the Sun."

Claire spun out her scant knowledge of the city's origins, before leading the way ahead.

Many times in the past, she had observed official guides holding aloft an umbrella or a newspaper to halt their party. Now, nearing the Abbey, she timidly raised her own arm.

"We're very proud of our fifteenth-century Abbey." Trying to sound like an authoritative native, she hoped her voice was carrying sufficiently now.

Faltering, she paused.

"P . . . perhaps," she stammered, "you would like a little time to browse inside. Meet me here in . . ." Claire consulted her watch in what she hoped was a professional manner. "Shall we say twenty minutes?"

T O her relief, the group, that is all except the lanky American, drifted away inside the Abbey's huge, wooden doors.

Drained of emotion, she flopped against the outer wall.

"Rather longer than necessary, I'd say." Brad grinned irritatingly. "Still that does give us time to grab a cup of tea."

She bridled at his audacity. "Wouldn't you rather see the interior?"

"I've seen it before, thanks."

"How long have you been in Bath then?" Claire asked testily.

Brad didn't reply. Instead he tucked his hand firmly beneath her elbow and guided her through the crowds towards a nearby tea-room.

"Now then," he said, when they were settled comfortably at a table, "tell me all about yourself."

With his cheerful chatter, Brad soon swept aside Claire's brief aggravation. Wary of giving herself away though, she spoke cautiously, dreading that he might probe too closely the subject of her "job."

Turning the tables, after a while she asked him some questions, but suspected his answers to be evasive. Perhaps he, too, had something to hide.

Eventually, it was the discovery that they were both fans of the same pop group that gently paved the way to friendship.

BACK outside the cafe, the group had re-assembled. Sensing their impatience, Claire recognised that Brad had been correct in his assumption that a 20-minute break was too long.

Groaning inwardly at the thought of continuing with this farce, she forced a smile, motioning her audience to gather round her.

Though completely out of context, she then related remembered snippets from her school-days about Beau Nash, once Bath's fashionable master of ceremonies.

Her audience listened attentively, their animated expressions temporarily lifting her confidence. A gentle hum of discussion spread throughout the party as they moved on.

"Poulteney Bridge, designed by Robert Adam," she announced with a flourish a little later.

Half-remembered facts lingered like limpets in the crevices of Claire's mind. As she prised each one free, the party pushed forward, their hands caressing the bridge's mellow stone as they leaned over the side to view the picturesque weir and gardens below.

"When?"

The question from an elderly lady at her side hit Claire like a bolt from the blue.

"Pardon?" Completely surrounded now, she didn't have the gall to consult the guide-book again.

"When was Poulteney Bridge designed?" the elderly lady persisted.

The minutes ticking away in silence, Claire looked blankly at the sea of expectant faces.

Just as she was about to panic, Brad took a step forward.

"It was 1771," he said quietly.

An inaudible sigh of relief escaping her lips, Claire averted her eyes away from his amused glance.

"Well done." Her tone was light, suggesting almost that she had set a deliberate memory test.

"What sort of stone was used?" was the next question, this time from a young man.

"Was that the same Robert Adam who designed furniture?" someone else called out.

Faced with several queries that she was unable to answer, Claire's face reddened. As the silence lengthened she flashed a beseeching look at Brad, but this time, he did not come to her rescue.

The group fidgeted and began talking amongst themselves.

A genuine guide would probably have smiled pleasantly and apologised for not knowing all the answers, but for Claire, acutely conscious of her bogus position, it all suddenly became too much. Her nerve failed.

She looked hopefully towards the busy street. The traffic lights were just changing and the green man flickered, signifying that it was safe to cross.

Taking her chance, she fled across the road, leaving the shocked tourists behind her.

"Claire!" Just before the traffic re-started, she heard Brad's urgent cry carrying on the breeze.

Tears of humiliation trickled down her cheeks as, scattering pigeons and pushing aside inquisitive shoppers, she ran through a cobbled square.

FINALLY, finding an empty wooden seat, in a less crowded area, Claire slumped down and searched through her shoulder-bag for a handkerchief.

It was absurd, she told herself, that she should attempt such a deception in order to spend a little time in the company of a man she had only just met. The best thing she could do now was to go home and try to forget all about it.

Claire gave herself a little time to recover, then dabbed her face discreetly with her powder puff. She was about to set off for the railway station, when she saw Brad hurrying towards her.

Blushing furiously, she lowered her head, too ashamed to meet his gaze.

Breathing heavily as though he'd been running, Brad sat down beside her. He reached out, taking her hand in his.

"Are you OK?"

Claire nodded.

"I feel so stupid," she murmured. "I can't think what made me pretend that I was a tour guide."

Not strictly the truth, but maybe later, she would tell him that it was her birthday, explain her feelings, laugh with him about the horoscope.

For now, she lifted her head a little and said shamefacedly, "I hope my behaviour hasn't spoilt your holiday in any way . . "

She paused, waiting for some reaction. When none came she continued, "I think you saw through me from the start."

Brad nodded and gave her hand a squeeze.

"I've a confession to make too," he said sheepishly. "I'm not on holiday. I've lived in Bath since I was a kid."

Seeing Claire's indignant expression, he shrugged apologetically. "I guess I just never lost my American accent."

She swallowed her surprise, then shuddered as other worries crowded into her mind.

"Whatever must all those people have thought of me?"

"I explained as best I could." Brad hesitated, shifting his position uncertainly. "They were very good about it."

His words came haltingly. "Their main concern seemed to be that I might not find you again . . ."

"Why should they care?" Claire interrupted, genuinely puzzled.

Brad looked embarrassed. "The romantics amongst them said they sensed our mutual attraction. I guess they were right about me . . ."

He leaned forward, his blue eyes inquiring.

Claire's heart-beat quickened and the phrase, "Love at first sight," popped unexpectedly into her mind.

"They were right," she admitted shyly, the tension gradually slipping away from her.

THEY sat for a while, holding hands and soaking up the midday sun.

"Mutual attraction," Claire laughed softly, beginning to see the funny side of it, "can cause an awful lot of trouble. One look at you and see what happened to me."

"My weird sense of humour is really to blame. People usually laugh at my jokes," Brad admitted. "There you were, standing right beside the tour notice with your guide-book in your hand. I just couldn't resist taking the mickey and asking if you were the guide."

He grimaced playfully, shrugging his shoulders. "It was only after you looked up, flashing those big green eyes at me. Somehow everything got out of hand.

"Before I knew what was happening you were leading the way round Bath. I should never have allowed it to go that far, but by then I was afraid that you might not see the joke and might be offended."

"Supposing I had pulled it off, and had completed the tour satisfactorily," Claire chipped in. "What then?"

For some time, she had had her suspicions about his role in the fiasco.

Brad laughed. "I'd have said exactly the same to you then as I'm going to say now."

A boyish expression on his face, he pointed to his wrist-watch. "I'm hungry, let's go and get something to eat."

He rose and with two hands pulled Claire to her feet, momentarily holding her near.

Grinning, he added, "I know all the best places."

Claire, savouring the thought that there would be ample opportunity for romance later, resisted the urge to linger in Brad's arms. Instead she stepped back, looking him squarely in the face.

"You do?"

His eyes danced wickedly and a puckish smile hovered on his lips.

"Of course," he quipped. "That's one of the reasons why . . ."

He flipped over the lapel of his casual jacket, indicating a badge pinned to the underside, and whispered, "*I'm* the official tour guide." □

IT was silly to get so excited about meeting someone you hadn't seen for eight years, Cindy Harkins sternly tried to reason with herself.

But her fingers paid no heed as her hand holding the lipstick trembled. She took several deep breaths, grasped the container firmly, and managed to apply it without smearing.

Then she heard the car drawing up at the gate and ran to the window, against which the autumn rain was pattering.

Two tall men got out, one slim and the other with a thickening waistline, and from her vantage point looking down, she noticed his hair was thinning, too.

Immediately, her attention was avidly on the slimmer man. But even after a gap of eight years in London, George Hislop's features could not have changed that much.

As they opened the gate, her gaze went to the stouter figure.

He looked up and caught sight of her at the bedroom window, grinned and gave her a wave. Without a doubt he was George Hislop.

Crisis For Cindy!

by BARBARA COWAN

D

C INDY stared for a moment in disbelief, stifling her disappointment, and gave a vigorous wave in return, as he then ran up the path towards shelter.

Suddenly, the happy glow she had felt for a week, since she knew George would be dropping in for dinner with a friend, died quietly. Once more she was back to reality.

Probably her father's muted reaction to the visit was wiser after all.

Her eye fell on the photograph on the dressing-table of herself at 16, with her 20-year-old twin sisters.

They stood with the slim, energetic-looking George, who smiled self-confidently into the camera. Eight years had changed him from this lithe, athletic figure to budding middle-age.

No-one knew she had a romantic side. She hid it well under a business-like exterior. But now the romantic half of her wanted to weep, while the sensible part mocked her stupidity.

Just this once she had let her romantic side take over. Secretly, she dreamed that since her two beautiful sisters were now happily married, the Gorgeous George, as the twins called him, would look at her with admiring eyes.

Jessica and Davina could afford to be very flippant about their admirers. Her widowed father used to grumble about them hanging around the house.

Yet, Cindy always thought George was different, not just because the others were local and he had the glamour of coming from London. He seemed to sense her shyness and how self-conscious she became when her flamboyant grandmother referred to her as "dear, plain, little Cindy."

Cindy sighed. Her foolish daydreams had evaporated in seconds. Gorgeous George had become the comfortably-rounded George.

"Cindy! Cindy! George has arrived!" Her gran's voice came to her from downstairs.

"Coming, Gran!"

She smoothed down the special red shirt she'd bought with such

▶ *over*

PITTENWEEM, FIFE

This picturesque fishing port was created a royal burgh in 1542, and is popular with artists and photographers. Near the harbour is the cave-shrine of St Fillan, which fell into disrepute when it was used by smugglers, but was rededicated in 1938. There are also the ruins of a 12th–century priory and the parish church with its tower, which dates from 1592. Pittenweem is one of the small towns in what is known as the East Neuk of Fife, described by King James VI as "a beggar's mantle fringed with gold."

PITTENWEEM, FIFE : J CAMPBELL KERR

care. It was simple and expensive, setting off her well-cut, silky, brown hair.

GEORGE and his colleague were standing looking up at her as she ran blithely downstairs, a slim, neat figure.

"Cindy! Little Cindy! You've become the real beauty of the family!" George bellowed, enveloping her in a brotherly bear hug.

Cindy's spirits rose. George might look different, but he was still the same jolly person who always took time to speak to her, even when the twins were around.

She realised now this was the real George. Her dreams were for someone who existed only in her romantic imagination.

George introduced her to his companion, Robert Vincent, who smiled politely, and shook her hand. He was much older than she had first thought.

The last little nail was driven into the coffin of her dreams when George revealed that Mr Vincent was his prospective father-in-law.

"Oh, how lovely!" Gran cooed over-enthusiastically. "And about time too, George. You've matured out of all recognition. Come into the lounge and tell us all about this lucky, lucky girl."

With a pang of embarrassment, Cindy instinctively realised that her grandmother, too, had been romanticallly linking George to her. Of course, Gran was dedicated to pushing eligible men into her path.

Smile and keep calm, Cindy told herself. This was just the same as dealing with a difficult situation in their chemist's shop, where she was manageress. It was a near-institution in their small, Moray, coast town, as it had been in the family since her grandfather's day.

She walked jauntily into the lounge, inquiring brightly as to what they wanted to drink before the meal. She would dispense, since it would be another half an hour before her father arrived home from the pharmacy.

Then, with her grandmother, she asked all the correct questions about the surveying job that had brought George and Mr Vincent so far north.

"Sorry to interrupt, but I think something in the kitchen is burning," Mr Vincent murmured, stopping Cindy and her grandmother in mid flow.

Mrs Harkins shrieked, "The pie! The pie! It'll be ruined!"

"Not to worry, Gran," Cindy quickly soothed her. "I'll see to it."

It was important to keep Gran away from cooking disasters in the kitchen. She became so upset that she was incapable of making another meal.

"Oh, yes — thank you, dear!" Gran agreed at once. "I'll leave you to sort things out."

She gratefully sank back in her chair.

As Cindy hurried out, she cringed as she heard Gran add, "Cindy wasn't blessed with the looks of her sisters, but she's such a competent girl, a real treasure in an emergency. She's quite famous hereabouts for carrying on in the family tradition."

Crisis For Cindy!

IN the kitchen, a blue haze of smoke came from the oven. The steak and kidney pie, Gran's choice of menu for cool autumn evenings, was a blackened mass. The apple crumble underneath was a bubbling blob of burnt sugar. Thank goodness, at least the soup was simmering gently on top of the cooker.

Cindy opened the back door and put the ruined food outside in the rain, the smoke stinging her eyes and throat.

The kitchen gradually cleared, and Cindy knew there would have to be a change of menu. Luckily, her father was a keen angler and there were a good number of fat, brown trout in the freezer.

Cindy dived into the freezer to take them out.

They could be stuffed and finished with a sprinkling of almonds, she decided. A salad would go well with them.

She ran to the kitchen phone — with luck she'd catch her father before he left — but another male voice answered.

It startled Cindy, especially when he went on cheerfully, "Ah, hello, Miss Harkins — Chris McLeod here. Your father has gone and I'm locking up for him."

Cindy recognised the new pharmacist who had only worked with them for a few months. He was a stranger from Glasgow, but very capable, coping with the summer influx of visitors and tourists.

He had impressed her father, but he stayed aloof from the usual shop backchat and gossip. It annoyed the unattached assistants, for he was single and a very personable young man.

Cindy had only exchanged words with him about business, for he was as coolly offhand as she was. Now his breezy manner seemed out of character.

"Are there any of the girls around?" Cindy asked urgently. "I need one of them to go next door to the supermarket for salad things and ice-cream."

"All gone home!" he murmured, then asked with quiet impertinence, "Are the steak pie and apple crumble progressing well for the Gorgeous George?"

"How did you know about that?" she gasped.

"I've heard the discussions over the past week. I'm not deaf," he replied, chuckling.

She remembered discussing tonight's visit quite openly with the other girls. Cindy felt her colour rise. Did he guess she had dreamed dreams about George?

"Then you'll realise I'm anxious to see George and his future father-in-law have a good meal," she said sharply.

"So there are in-laws on George's horizon — good!" he remarked. He went on conversationally, "Do I take it there's been a mishap with the food?"

"Yes," she snapped. Then she saw the comical side of the situation. "The pie and crumble are presently outside the back door quietly incinerating themselves," she explained.

"Ah yes, I know the position well," he murmured. "So now more

▶ p 56

BEN LOYAL AND THE KYLE OF TONGUE, SUTHERLAND : J CAMPBELL KERR

provisions are urgently required. I'll undertake to procure them for you — on one condition!"

Cindy blinked, not sure if she had heard correctly.

"One — one condition, did you say?" she queried.

"Yes — that you set another place and invite me to dinner."

Cindy heard his suppressed chuckle and found she was smiling, too. She decided to call his bluff.

"Certainly," she said heartily. "But on my conditions . . ."

"Yes, I'm listening!"

"The following goods must be here within the next half-hour."

She went on to detail her requests.

"No problem!" he said cheerfully, after he had read back the list to double-check it.

Cindy put down the phone, stifling a little giggle. That young man didn't know what he had let himself in for, she thought. Just wait till her grandmother went to work on him. Gran would immediately see him as husband material for her unmarried granddaughter.

CHRIS MCLEOD, you'll be sorry!" she sang under her breath, as she hurried to set another place.

Then she paused, smiling. Now she was looking forward to Chris McLeod coming, when an hour ago it was George. Yet, she did like Chris's sense of fun. Amazing, he'd never revealed it before — but then she'd never given him a chance till now.

Just then she heard her father coming in at the front door, and knew he'd be pleased. Several times he'd hinted that the new pharmacist must be invited for a meal. Chris would help make his evening more enjoyable.

George's voice was booming out from the lounge.

Strange, what eight years had made her forget — George's voice used to annoy her father. Dad would find it a trial, especially when he hadn't been enthusiastic when Gran gave out the invitation for dinner in the first place.

The trout were quickly defrosted in the microwave, and she was just finishing their preparation for the oven when there was a knock

---

BEN LOYAL AND THE KYLE OF TONGUE, SUTHERLAND

Sometimes called the Queen of the Scottish Peaks, Ben Loyal has four distinctively sculptured tops. Until 1972, the only way to reach Melness, to the west of the Kyle of Tongue, from Tongue on the eastern shore, was to travel right round the Kyle. Then a causeway was built as part of the main coastal road, although the old road still provides a pleasant route for those in no hurry.

◀p 55

on the back door. She found Chris McLeod standing, both hands occupied with bulging plastic shopping bags, rain dripping off his hair and mac.

He didn't wait to be invited in, but brushed past her and heaved the bags on to the kitchen table.

"All the bits and pieces you asked for," he announced cheerfully, "and some extras over and above. Thought I should contribute to the meal since I forced myself on you."

He grinned, and dived into the bags bringing out the lettuce, salad goods and ice-cream she had asked for, followed by a huge, Black Forest gâteau.

"That can replace the crumble," he said. "And here are some cheeses and biscuits for those who prefer them."

He piled up small packages on the table.

"I'm very grateful for your thoughtfulness," Cindy murmured, trying to think of how to treat this young man.

She could not be as coolly offhand as usual, since he had done so much to help — and he'd got soaked collecting the shopping. She fetched a towel for him while he peeled off his raincoat, and then waited while he rubbed his hair dry.

"Come and I'll introduce you to George and —" she started.

"No, no! I'll give you a hand to get things ready. I know your father doesn't like his evening meal delayed past seven-thirty. That's his deadline, he told me."

Cindy could only nod agreement. Her father got very cross if he was kept waiting for his dinner.

"Would you wash the salad things?" she asked tentatively.

He nodded and took his jacket off, then rolled up his sleeves and draped a towel apron-wise round his waist.

Cindy put the stuffed trout into a low oven, and the potatoes on to boil, feeling a little bemused. She was very aware of this fair-haired, blue-eyed man busy at the sink, humming under his breath.

He seemed to be coping super-efficiently as she laid the empty salad bowls at his elbow. He nodded and started at once to fill them with competent swiftness.

"Worked in hotel kitchens as a student," he explained, when she gasped at his skill.

She found herself laughing at his unexpected professional short-cuts. They worked quickly together and any remaining awkwardness soon melted away.

As they were just finishing, her grandmother came into the kitchen.

"Why, Mr McLeod, I didn't expect to find you here . . ." She stared amazed at Chris, the towel still wrapped round his waist.

"Brought round the goods for the change in menu — and stayed to help." Chris smiled. "I must say Cindy and I make a great team in the kitchen."

"Oh, how kind!" Seeing Cindy being pleasant to a young man delighted Mrs Harkins and she smiled sweetly at Chris.

"Since you've done so much of the work you must stay for dinner, then." She beamed.

"I'd love to!"

"Lovely! Lovely! I'll get everyone to the table now since you're ready to serve. That son of mine is becoming quite tetchy." Mrs Harkins bustled out.

"You certainly know how to handle my grandmother," Cindy observed, as Chris started to take off the towel and put on his jacket.

"Oh yes, we've met before! She came round to the shop in my first week and told me all about your good points in great detail. But she kept calling you 'dear, plain little Cindy,' for some reason."

"Oh no!" Cindy wailed, closing her eyes in near despair. "She thinks I was deprived because I wasn't born tall and a red-head like her side of the family."

"Red-heads are very nice, but for preference give me a neat brunette, wearing a red shirt just like yours." Chris grinned. "Anyway, all the locals told me she did it, and how it annoyed you."

He lined up the soup bowls, then continued, "I soon discovered that you were very cool and distant towards young men — although you've got all the gentlemen pensioners eating out of your hand, and even the schoolboys think you're great."

Suddenly, Cindy started to giggle. "You really are a very forward young man, as my grandmother would say."

"No, I'm just honest — and patient. I knew an occasion like this would turn up, and just bided my time!" he murmured, setting the filled bowls on a tray.

"Cindy! Would you pass through the soup! We're waiting!" Her father appeared at the serving hatch.

Then he saw Chris. "Oh good, you've come after all!"

"Yes, Mrs Harkins gave me an invitation, too. I just couldn't refuse," Chris murmured, and winked towards Cindy.

"Coming, Dad!" she cried, and carried the tray over, smiling widely.

She couldn't believe it! This was real — not a dream — not even a daydream. Chris had sought her out completely on his own initiative.

Gran would take the credit, no matter what. She always did! But did it matter?

Not a jot, Cindy thought, especially at this moment when she felt so happy! □

BROCKHAMPTON HALL, HEREFORDSHIRE

Built around 1400, this timber-framed manor house is now owned by the National Trust. It's in a picturesque area noted for Hereford cattle — and for cider apples!

BROCKHAMPTON HALL, HEREFORDSHIRE : J CAMPBELL KERR

Divided—

SANDY glared at the stack of property agent's details spread out across the kitchen table, certain now that the house did not exist which would appeal both to her and Dan.

He'd stormed off to the office 10 minutes ago without so much as a goodbye, leaving her with tears of rage welling in her eyes. This special time, which was supposed to be so full of joy and anticipation, was turning into a nightmare.

Even trying to think of the unborn child, growing inside her, which as yet didn't show, failed to calm her shattered nerves. With a heavy sigh, she picked up her bag and headed for the door.

Perhaps they were meant to spend the rest of their lives living in this flat, she thought gloomily. It had been perfect for the two of them, but would be quite impossible with a baby.

The row this morning had been about the new development outside town — spanking new houses with all mod-cons, fitted kitchens, central heating, small, square gardens, and absolutely no character whatsoever.

"They've no character because they're not lived in," Dan had protested. "Just look at this! Most women would give their right arm for a fitted kitchen like it! And it wouldn't take us long to make the garden look pretty."

"I don't want to live on an estate," she'd said stubbornly. "I still don't see what was wrong with the house on Victoria Avenue."

"Well, nothing, if you discount the fact that half the roof was missing, it had dry rot and plaster was falling off the walls in handfuls."

by TERESA ASHBY

We Stand!

"There was one slate missing! And it had character!"

They had the same old arguments over and over again. They trailed around houses in their lunch-hour, and while Dan enthused energetically, Sandy would sigh with disinterest.

In the houses Sandy liked, Dan would poke at dubious pieces of woodwork or stamp on sick-sounding floorboards, jotting down notes which he kept and later used in evidence against her!

SANDY hesitated at the door, then turned back and, gathering up the details, put them into her bag. Some of them had only come in the morning's post — perhaps there was something there worth a second look.

At work, Dan called her.

"I'm sorry about this morning," he said.

"Me, too." She felt relieved that he'd bothered to call.

"It was stupid to walk out on you like that. We'll go through those details again tonight . . ."

"There's no point," she said miserably. "The houses are all old. I've looked through them. That only leaves the estate."

"They must have been new once," he reminded her, "and probably bare and cold. I'm going to have a look at those new houses at lunch-time. Won't you come with me?"

She bit her lip.

"I — I'm taking a late lunch," she said.

There was no need to tell him that she had arranged a late appointment to view a house. She was clutching at straws going to see it, the same way that he was clutching at straws by going to the new development.

"I'll see you at home, then," he said. " 'Bye, Sandy."

She hung up and looked at the photograph at the top of the duplicated sheet of paper. It was the kind of house she'd always dreamed of owning. As she read through the details, she could almost hear Dan's objections.

Thatched roof. "Oh, for goodness' sake, Sandy! It'd be full of spiders and bats and mice! It'd cost a fortune to insure and maintain."

Large country garden. "That means overgrown, Sandy. Can you cope with a wilderness? I know I can't."

Farmhouse kitchen. "One cupboard and an ancient, wood-burning stove."

Cosy sitting-room. "Pokey!"

And there was, of course, the price to consider. For the same amount of money, they could buy one of the brand-new houses with all the extras — carpets, kitchen equipment and so on.

Several times during the morning, she almost called to cancel her appointment, knowing it was hopeless even going to see the house. She doubted if she'd ever get Dan even to read the details, no matter how much she loved it.

Tears began to prick at her eyes again. After all, it was she who was going to spend all day, every day, living there! If she was forced to live in some modern monstrosity, then — then she might as well stay right here in the flat!

G EORGINA CARPENTER got up from her chair at the sound of the doorbell and hobbled down the hall. The appointment was early, she thought grumpily. She had hoped to have a nap before she had to start showing people around the house.

"Oh," she said when she opened the door to a young man. She had been expecting a woman.

"I'm sorry to bother you." He grinned so charmingly that she forgot to be cross. "I was just passing and I saw the sale sign in the garden."

"Did you also see that it said, 'Strictly by appointment only'?" she rebuked him.

"I'm sorry," he apologised again. "I'll call the agents and — "

"No, that won't be necessary," she said. "But before I let you in, could I see some proof of identity?"

"Of course." He rifled through his pockets and pulled out his driving licence. "I am registered with the agents," he added. "Why don't you call them and check?"

"Would you mind waiting there while I do that?" she said, and closed the door.

She felt a little silly going to such extremes, but her daughter had impressed upon her the need to be careful.

"Like it or not, you're vulnerable living alone, Mother," she'd said. "I promise, no genuine caller will mind you doing a little checking-up."

The young man didn't mind either. When she opened up the front door again, he was examining the shrubs in the front garden.

"Do you like gardening, Mr Turner?" she said.

"I'm not sure," he admitted.

"This may be a big garden," she told him, "but it's very easy to maintain. I've been finding it increasingly difficult, though, with my arthritis."

"You'll be sorry to leave," he prompted, following her into the hall.

"Yes, in a way," she said. "I've lived here all my married life, but I'll be moving in with my daughter and her family.

"One has to take a positive approach to these situations. When living alone becomes a worry instead of a pleasure, I think it's time to move on, don't you?"

"Do you have any trouble with the roof?" he asked.

"People always want to know that!" She laughed. "Everyone seems to think it must be infested with mice and rats and goodness knows what else! Like everything it has advantages and disadvantages. For one thing, it's very warm."

She showed him round, careful to keep an eye on the time. He was impressed, she could see that. She was proud of her house — it was pleasant, neat and clean. There were the odd one or two things that needed seeing to, but it was basically sound.

When they'd finished, she expected him to say what everyone else said: "I'll get in touch with the agents."

They all said that, but she hadn't had a single offer yet. To her surprise, he put in a bid there and then. It was a little less than her asking price, but she had always been prepared to negotiate.

"I'm very keen to buy this," he said.

"I'm sorry, I can't possibly give you an answer." Georgina Carpenter shook her head. "I'm expecting a young lady this afternoon. I really should let her see it before making any decision."

"If she fails to meet the asking price, would you get in touch with me?" he said urgently. "This house really means a lot to me. It's by far the most suitable I've seen."

He looked desperate.

► *over*

Glorious Gardens
Culzean Castle, Strathclyde

LIKE Robert Adam's architectural masterpiece, Culzean's gardens are on a grand scale. The formal fountain court, begun at the same time, blends happily with its parapets and terraces. The parklands beyond were landscaped, and boast fine trees and picturesque views.

Later owners of Culzean also made their mark, adding a Gothick camellia house, a swan pond (complete with charming cottage for the keeper), and a notable collection of plants, from giant firs to exotic palms and bamboo.

"I won't make any decisions without speaking to you first." She smiled. "But I'm not making any promises."

With any luck, she thought, the young lady this afternoon wouldn't make an offer. She quite liked the idea of the house going to someone who appreciated it.

SANDY parked outside the house and stopped for a moment to look at it. It was quite the most beautiful house she'd ever seen.

The pink-painted walls, nestling beneath the thatched roof, seemed to glow warmly in the afternoon sun. She closed her eyes for a moment and pictured herself pushing a pram along this sunny road, or working in the garden while the baby played in the play-pen.

A dream, that's all it was, just a forlorn dream.

The old lady who answered the door looked tired. Sandy thought she must be very sad to be leaving a house like this.

"Hello, dear, you're punctual," Mrs Carpenter remarked. "Come along in."

In every room, Sandy could picture herself living here. She could see the baby playing in the sunny patch on the living-room carpet, could see herself working in the roomy kitchen. The trouble was, whenever she pictured them living here, Dan was absent from the scene.

He wouldn't fit a place like this any better than she would fit a modern house. She did the only thing she could do — she forced herself to see it through Dan's eyes.

"There's a patch of damp here, Mrs Carpenter," she said, and the old lady's lips tightened.

"A gentleman who looked over the cottage earlier said that it would be quite easily remedied," she pointed out, stressing the word gentleman.

"I didn't mean — " Sandy began, but Mrs Carpenter was already going up the stairs.

Sandy paused at the top. A floorboard had squealed and she stepped back on it, just the way Dan would, testing it with her heel.

"There's nothing wrong with these floors," Mrs Carpenter said crossly. "The nice gentleman who looked round earlier said that they felt perfectly solid!"

Sandy's heart fell when she saw the bathroom. Instead of the modern suite she knew Dan would prefer, there was an old bath with claw feet.

"You'd have to pay a lot of money to get a bath of that quality these days," Mrs Carpenter said proudly.

The more Sandy saw, the more hopeless she realised this was. One of the window-sills was rotten and, despite Mrs Carpenter's assurances that her "gentleman" said it was a minor repair, Sandy knew that as far as Dan was concerned, it would mean new windows for the whole place.

E

"The garden's so big," she breathed, looking down on it from an upstairs window.

She imagined a rope swing down there in the orchard, a hammock on the wavy-edged lawn, a sand-pit in the shelter of the gnarled oak . . .

She thought it was quite the most beautiful garden she had ever seen in her life, but she said, "My goodness, it must require a lot of work to keep it looking so nice."

"Oh, I trot out with my shears from time to time and run the electric mower over the grass, but — " Mrs Carpenter broke off, the young woman was clearly not listening.

"Tell me," Mrs Carpenter said. "Do you like the house?"

"It's just lovely," Sandy's eyes filled with tears. "But my husband — we were looking for something a little more modern."

"I see." Mrs Carpenter sniffed. "One of those boxes on the hill, I suppose! It's all right if you like that kind of thing. As it happens, the gentleman who called this morning made me an offer. I was simply waiting until you'd seen the house before accepting it."

As she drove away, Sandy told herself over and over again that it didn't matter where they lived. Four walls and a roof were all they needed. The important thing was that they were together, and that the baby was born healthy and happy.

Resolutely, she drove on up to the new estate. It didn't seem to matter that she'd be late for work. It was time to stop dreaming and get down to reality.

The houses were nicer than she'd imagined and not all identical as she'd feared.

"It will all look much better once this area has been turfed," the sales officer said as they stepped across a plank and in through the front door.

She tried to imagine the small garden filled with flowering shrubs, but, each time, all she could see was the wonderful cottage garden with all its secret corners and old, established plants.

The kitchen was small, but stuffed to capacity with oak-fronted units and built-in everything. Even the waste paper bin was built into a cupboard.

"You'll find you're never short of storage space," she was told.

The bedrooms, too, had a wealth of fitted cupboards. The window frames were all rot-proof plastic and double-glazed. "Saving considerably on heating bills," the sales officer reminded her, as would the cavity wall insulation.

It was a nice house, she thought, as she left, a very nice house. Not a dream of a house, perhaps, but it had an awful lot of good points.

AT dinner that evening, Sandy and Dan were both subdued, having hardly exchanged two words since getting home from work. Dan was deep in thought, and Sandy was debating whether to burn her boats and admit that she'd seen one of the brand-new houses and quite liked it.

"Look, Sandy," Dan said suddenly, shattering the silence. "We've been looking at houses all over the place ever since we knew there was a baby on the way. If we're going to get in and settled before it's born, then we must make some kind of decision soon."

"I agree," she said.

He looked startled, making her wonder if she'd really become so predictably unreasonable.

"I mean, a lot of these older houses need money spent on them and — "

BLONDE BOMBSHELL

Oh dear! What can the matter be,
Am I imagining friends disapprove
of me?
Trying their best not to stare?
Could it be envy
This faint animosity,
Critical, kindly, or
Pure curiosity?
Why should I feel like a
Walking atrocity —
For changing the shade
Of my hair!

— Gemma Gaye.

"I know," she interrupted. "A modern house would be more economical and easier to keep clean. It's the sensible answer to our problems."

His mouth dropped open, and Sandy smiled. She must be confusing him with her sudden change of heart. She'd been doing a lot of thinking today, and had come to realise that all Dan wanted was the very best for them.

He licked his lips and put down his knife and fork. "The thing is, I've seen a house I like and I've paid the agents a holding deposit," he confessed.

Sandy knew she should feel annoyed that he was being so high-handed, but she couldn't bring herself to object.

"Fine," she said.

He looked astounded. "Fine?" he repeated.

"What do you want me to say?" she asked sadly.

"I don't want to browbeat you, Sandy," he said softly, reaching across the table to take her hand in his. "I'm only doing what I think is best. I'm sure you'll like the house, too. I wouldn't have said we'd have it if I thought otherwise. Trust me, Sandy."

She smiled as the love inside her created a warm glow. It didn't matter whether the house was old or new, they'd make it theirs. It might even be fun, creating a garden from scratch, creating a home from their own imaginations.

"I'll take you to see it tomorrow at lunch-time," he said.

"I'll look forward to it," she promised. She hadn't mentioned that she'd already looked at the houses on the estate. It didn't seem necessary, somehow.

THE following day, the sun still shone. Sandy sat in the passenger seat, wishing that Dan had taken a different route. This way would take them right past the cottage.

As they drew closer, she saw that the Sale sign had had a large "Sold" sticker pasted across it. So Mrs Carpenter had agreed to sell it to her "gentleman."

"Is something wrong with the car?" she said as Dan pulled up outside the cottage.

"No." He was grinning like a mischievous child. "Come on, out you get."

Slowly, numb with disbelief, she got out of the car and, with her hand enclosed firmly within Dan's, she allowed herself to be led through the gate and into the garden.

"It needs a little work," he whispered, "but only a very little. There's nothing wrong that I can't put right myself."

"But . . ."

"As soon as I saw it," he went on, "I thought of you. I could see you here, Sandy, and as I looked around, I could see us all here. It's a lovely house. I know we can be happy here."

They paused in the front garden, and Sandy couldn't speak for the lump in her throat. When she looked at Dan, he was looking at the house with genuine enthusiasm.

He really did like it! He wasn't faking anything.

"Shall we go inside?" He smiled and she nodded.

Mrs Carpenter opened the door, and her startled look quickly vanished when Dan introduced them.

"This is my wife," he said. "I'd like to show her round."

"Of course!" Mrs Carpenter smiled and aimed a wink in Sandy's direction.

"For its age, this house is in excellent condition," he said knowledgeably. "Mrs Carpenter tells me that the heating bills are remarkably low, thanks to the insulating properties of the thatch. And, let's face it, we won't have to worry about slates flying off the roof each time there's a storm!"

While they looked around the house, Mrs Carpenter made a pot of tea.

"Do you like it?" she asked Sandy when they came back.

"I love it," Sandy said simply, and Dan squeezed her hand. "We both do," she added.

"Good!" Mrs Carpenter beamed. "If you're half as happy here as I've been, then you're in for a wonderful time!"

Sandy didn't doubt it. This house really did have everything — character, low maintenance. It only remained for them to add that own special ingredient of their own — love. That was going to be the easiest part of all . . . □

by KATE
CLAYTON

Apologies All Round...

"THERE'S a rumour going around," Nick said, "about your father and a certain lady."

"It's not a rumour," I told him bitterly. "It's true — worse luck."

We were walking home from college together, which was my favourite part of the day.

"Why so sour?" Nick queried. "It's ages since your mother died."

I didn't reply for a minute, then I said, "D'you know Mrs Hamiton?"

"I'll say I do. She used to teach me when I was in the Infants. She's tops."

"It's easy for you to say that," I retorted. "She's not going to be your stepmother."

"Come off it, Pen," he said with a touch of the temper that went with his red hair. "Surely your dad deserves a bit of the good life. He's not all that old!"

"He's in his forties!"

Nick gave a most exasperating sigh. "You know, Pen, you really are quite naive. Why don't you grow up a bit?

"If you expect to do well in this Drama Course you're taking at college, you should develop a bit of empathy — if you know what that is."

I could have hit him. "Of course I know what empathy is. It's being able to understand what makes people tick."

"Exactly," Nick said. "Your own father, for instance."

"How would you like to have your life taken over by a stepmother?" I demanded.

"Mrs Hamilton wouldn't do that. As a family we know her well. Mum likes her no end. Why can't you?"

"She's so soppy," I grumbled. "She treats him like a — a knight in armour. It's ridiculous at their age."

"Being older doesn't stop people falling in love," insisted Nick. "To her, your father probably seems like a knight in armour. As I said, you need to grow up."

"You're being horrible," I said. "For goodness' sake, let's change the subject."

"OK," he agreed, but all the friendliness had left his voice, and a chill settled in my heart. Nick was terribly important to me, and I hated to quarrel with him. But there were some things he just didn't understand, and I resented his criticism. He enjoyed a lovely family life with mother, father, two sisters and a brother. How could he feel empathy for me?

WE walked on in silence for a while, and I couldn't think of anything to say to put things right between us. We parted coolly, too, when we reached my home.

"Be seeing you," was all he said.

"Will you — will you be coming to the play reading tonight?" I faltered.

"Not sure," he said. "As you know, I'm doing props, and I've one or two items to round up this evening."

His voice softened a bit then. "I hope you get the part of Juliet. I know how much you want to do it."

"Thanks," I said. "It's a toss-up between Veronica Watson and me. What do you think?"

I waited eagerly for his reply.

"I don't know," he said. "I'm not sure if you could be really convincing — certainly not in your present mood. Juliet was a girl who understood about love."

"I hate you, Nick Moffat!" I shouted, and flounced off, leaving him standing in the middle of the road looking bewildered.

Moira Hamilton was in the kitchen — *my* kitchen. She didn't seem to realise it wasn't hers — yet — and was always popping in to cook something special for Dad!

"Hi, Penny," she called cheerily. "I thought I'd get supper started as you're off to the Drama Group tonight."

I know I should have said, "Thanks a lot." I was still smouldering from Nick's criticism, so I muttered an ungracious, "You shouldn't have bothered."

Moira didn't reply. She went on stirring whatever she had in the pot, and I went up to my room and studied my script.

The village Drama Group was putting on extracts from "Romeo And Juliet," and there were two of us in competition for the role of Juliet. I felt I should be chosen because I was actually studying Drama at college, and I had a stronger voice than Veronica Watson.

I also had long, blonde hair whereas she was a swarthy, boyish brunette.

I just needed to shed a few pounds to be worthy of the part, and I was doing slimming exercises when Dad called that supper was ready.

I hoped Moira Hamilton had remembered I was dieting. She was inclined to cook all sorts of exotic dishes to show off her prowess — to fatten Dad up, she said. Why should it matter to her that I worried about my weight?

To my dismay, she'd made a large steak and kidney pudding. It looked delicious, all soft and succulent with rich, brown gravy oozing from the bottom.

"I don't want any of that," I said, without fully realising how ungracious I must have sounded.

"Penny!" Dad exclaimed. "Where are your manners?"

ODE TO OUTFITS

There is something about a uniform,
Which is difficult to define,
It's not so much the colour,
Or the cut or shape or line.
It's a kind of splendid grandeur,
It's a neatness, it's a kit,
It's a dashing, smart distinction,
With its undisputed fit.
There's a striking manliness and strength,
A correctness and a pride,
Which makes a man impressive,
And transforms the male inside.
How I love all national costumes,
Mankind dressed up to the hilt,
But the one who make my knees go weak,
Is the Scot who wears a kilt!

— *Chrissy Greenslade.*

"She knows I'm trying to slim!" I yelled, glaring at Moira. "No-one cares what I want."

I burst into tears. I was so hungry and hurting inside I couldn't stay, so with a muttered, "Excuse me," I fled to the sanctuary of my room.

I flung myself on to the bed and had a real good weep. Today was the worst day of my whole life, I told myself, as I snuffled into my soaking pillow.

I must have dozed off, however, for when I woke up I realised I would be late for the Drama Group. I was, too — they had just about finished, and Mrs Marlow, who was looking after the costumes, met me in the cloakroom.

"We thought you weren't coming, Penny," she said. "We've already had a fitting session."

She had an exquisite dress hanging over her arm.

"Here," she said, "try it on quickly. It's Juliet's dress."

"Veronica has already tried it on and it's a shade big for her. I think it will be just fine on you."

But it wasn't! The back zip refused to pull up. It stuck at waist level, and Mrs Marlow gazed with dismay.

"Oh dear," she kept saying. "What can we do? Would you mind very much if we ask Veronica to play Juliet?"

Of course I minded! I minded desperately, but I couldn't say so, so instead I asked Mrs Marlow if I might take the dress home and see if I could alter it.

She was doubtful.

"It's a hired dress, you know," she said. "You'd have to take great care of it."

"I — might be able to — make it fit," I faltered miserably.

I was anticipating a week of complete starvation! Surely I would shrink then?

"Can you sew?" Mrs Marlow said, and I crossed my fingers and nodded.

WHEN I got home Dad and Moira were out. I'd forgotten they went to the Choral Society on Wednesday evenings.

On the kitchen table was a tray containing a crisp, little, salad meal and a note sighed, "Moira," which read, "Sorry, Penny. Please forgive. Love."

I ate the salad ravenously, then I went upstairs and tried on the Juliet dress again. It was so pretty with its banded Italian sleeves and sweetheart neckline; but the zip stuck just the same as before.

I stood in front of my wardrobe mirror in a state of complete dejection, and that's how Moira found me. She didn't notice the zip at first and her face broke into smiles.

"Why, Penny!" she exclaimed. "You got the part. I'm so happy for you."

"No," I gulped, "I haven't. The Juliet dress won't fit. It's too tight. Veronica Watson is a whole size smaller than I am, and Mrs Marlow says she'll have to be offered the part . . ."

Moira didn't say anything. She screwed up her eyes and bit her lip. Then she said, "Turn around, love."

I did, and she ran her fingers over the straining zip.

"I can make this dress fit, Penny. I'm sure of it. There's at least an inch on either side of each dart. If we let them out, it will make all the difference."

"Honestly?" I croaked.

"Honestly!"

She smiled and gave me a little hug, and I realised her face, though not exactly beautiful, was kind, and her eyes were shining with affection.

"Get your nail scissors out, Penny," she said, "and let's get started. There's no time like the present."

There we were, happily snipping stitches and talking together, when Dad put his head round the door.

"There's a red-headed guy downstairs asking for Penny. Funny type, he's got a lute on a cord hanging round his neck and what looks like half a balcony underneath each arm. Shall I send him away?"

"No! No!" I cried joyfully. "Please don't send him away. He's the happy ending to the most miserable day of my life."

My eyes met Moira's then, and she grinned a most understanding grin. I realised then that as well as the happy ending, there was going to be a happy new beginning! □

Glorious Gardens

Crathes Castle, Grampian

THIS fairy-tale castle presides over an enchanting series of eight separate gardens, divided by ancient yew hedges. Each garden has a different theme and a name to match — the Fountain Garden, Trough Garden, Camel Garden (with two humps), and so on.

Sir James and Lady Burnett were the last owners of Crathes before it was given to the National Trust for Scotland in 1951.

Music

For Two

by
AUDREY
GROOM

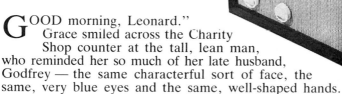

G OOD morning, Leonard."
Grace smiled across the Charity
Shop counter at the tall, lean man,
who reminded her so much of her late husband,
Godfrey — the same characterful sort of face, the
same, very blue eyes and the same, well-shaped hands.

But there the likeness ended. Godfrey wouldn't have known "Land
Of Hope And Glory" from "The Blue Danube."

This chap was very interested in music.

There'd been an old guitar for sale the other day in the shop, and
he'd picked it up and given them a little tune. He came in two or
three times a week to look through the records.

"Good morning, Grace." His eyes twinkled back at her. "I'm
making a special search today."

"Are you, Leonard? Well, this is the 'find everything' shop, you
know that. What are you after?'

"A record of an old song. You'll be too young to remember it, of
course, 'Little Grey Home In The West.' "

Grace laughed. "Too young, indeed — my mother used to sing
that."

"So did mine! That's why I want it. I came across the old sheet
music at home, but unfortunately, I've no longer a piano to play it
on, and I'd love to hear it."

"Well, maybe you'll be lucky. I'll keep a lookout anyway,
Leonard."

"Bless you."

He moved over to search through the pile of records in the corner,
while Grace took the money for some books from another customer.

She felt quite light-hearted. She always felt better for seeing
Leonard, somehow.

"No luck today," he said after a while. "I'll try again later in the week, Grace."

"Do, Leonard, do." She gave him a warm smile as he left the shop, and began to polish up the old glassware, so that it shone in the sunshine, like diamonds.

Grace really enjoyed working here. There had been so many empty hours to fill, she had found, since her husband had died three years back, so many empty hours that made the pain and the loneliness so much more poignant.

Then a couple of months back she had seen the advert for voluntary helpers in this shop, and life had really taken a turn for the better.

Grace enjoyed cleaning up the old, interesting things that came in for sale, and she loved chatting to the customers.

L EONARD came in again on Friday, looking as young and excited as a schoolboy.

"I've found it, Grace, I've found it. Went to our local church jumble sale last night and there it was, large as life — 'Little Grey Home In The West' on one side, and 'Somewhere A Voice Is Calling' on the other."

"Oh! Wonderful." Grace felt excited for him.

Then his face fell.

"The only trouble is now," he told her, "it's a 78 record. My equipment doesn't play 78s."

"Oh! That's a pity." Grace thought for a moment. "What you want, Leonard, is one of those old portable gramophones. We often get those in the shop."

"Do you? That would be marvellous. I tell you what then, Grace, I'm going down to London tomorrow to spend a couple of weeks with my daughter. If one comes in while I'm gone, could you save it for me?"

"Of course I will."

Grace felt only too pleased that if she wasn't to see his smiling face for a couple of weeks, she would at least have something interesting to concentrate on, especially as she knew how much it would please him if she found the elusive object.

"See you in about a fortnight then, Grace," he said, "probably the Monday after I come back."

"Have a lovely holiday," she told him.

Every day, bags and boxes of people's cast-offs, turned-outs, and no-longer-wanteds were deposited in the Charity Shop doorway.

It was sad, in some ways, Grace reflected. People seemed to tire of things so quickly nowadays. In another, it was exciting, knowing that one person's junk could be another's treasure, particularly if you were looking for something special, as she was.

Every large, square box raised her hopes — and brought them tumbling down again when each one turned out to be the wrong thing.

WHEN, just about a week after Leonard had left, there it was, an old record-player.

Marvellous! Grace carried it carefully to the back of the shop, and since there were no customers for the moment, she set about dusting and polishing it.

In fact, she became quite carried away by the job, and didn't even notice when Shirley Blackman, who was in charge, arrived.

Shirley was a practical woman and a keen worker, giving unstintingly of her time to good causes, but she had no feeling for the old things which passed through their hands, as Grace had.

"Not much point in polishing that, Grace," she said, as she hung up her coat. "It'll sell, clean or dirty — they usually do."

"Well, I'm keeping it for someone actually," Grace replied. "He'll be in on Monday week."

"You can't do that, Grace — it's not fair to other customers."

Grace was a little put off at Shirley's tone. That most people deferred to her, she was well aware.

She really couldn't over this, though. She folded her duster and gave Shirley a smile that indicated that, on this, she had made up her mind.

"Well, just for the week, Shirley," she said. "That'll be all right, won't it?"

Shirley pursed her lips and frowned, but obviously wasn't sufficiently concerned to make an issue of the matter at the moment.

She had seen a frail, little woman, standing in the shop with a dress over her arm, and strode through to tell her in a loud, authoritarian voice, what excellent value it was for the money.

Thank goodness, Grace thought. Since she was absolutely certain that Leonard would come the following Monday, she didn't imagine there would be any need for further confrontation.

Only, he didn't come.

Still, what's one day, Grace thought philosophically as she unlocked the shop on Tuesday morning. He'll come today.

But he didn't.

As further days passed and he still didn't come, there were rumblings of dissatisfaction from Shirley.

"Time you moved that thing into the front of the shop, Grace.

"People are very unreliable.

"You can't trust anyone to keep a promise these days."

Grace was depressed and disappointed. She just couldn't believe that Leonard would let her down.

Surprisingly, apart from the grumbles, Shirley was very patient. It wasn't until almost a month later, at closing time, that she issued her ultimatum.

"If that man hasn't turned up by Saturday, Grace, I'm putting that record-player in the window, and that's that."

Well, Grace thought, what can I say? We obviously can't keep it for ever.

Then, walking home, she had a bright idea. She could at least phone him and tell him the thing was there, couldn't she?

He had an unusual surname. He'd told it to her during one of their chats, and they'd laughed about it — Lemonson. Surely there couldn't be too many of those in the local telephone directory.

There he was, *Leonard Lemonson, 15 Brodick Crescent.*

Unfortunately, all she got on the line was a confused burr. So what was the next move? To walk round there.

Brodick Crescent — a nice road, with well-kept houses. Nine, eleven, thirteen, ah! Fifteen. Good gracious, it was empty. A *FOR SALE* board creaked on a post at the gate.

Grace stood and stared. He must have moved away, and he hadn't even been into the shop to tell her he'd changed his mind about the record-player, or to say goodbye.

DISAPPOINTMENT welled up in her and she felt all her age and a little bit more. In fact she would have quite liked to stay home the next day, but of course she couldn't.

Shirley depended on her, and in any case, there was something she must do.

"I think this has been at the back long enough," she said, carrying the record-player into the shop.

She was glad that Shirley only nodded, and didn't make a big issue of it.

What a cheerless day it was! No-one bought anything, no-one seemed to want to talk.

Then in the middle of the afternoon a lad came into the shop. Instead of homing in on the T-shirts and jeans, as the young usually did, he crouched down beside the record-player, and gave a whistle of approval.

"Nice little job this," he said to Grace. "How much is this, lady?"

She quoted him the price which Shirley had suggested, although she felt it too high, and he whistled again, and continued to examine it.

Although she knew it was utterly stupid, Grace found herself praying, "Don't buy it, young man, please don't buy it."

At that very moment, a tall figure entered the shop, and Grace thought she must be having hallucinations. But when she heard Leonard Lemonson's voice, she knew she wasn't.

"Hello, Grace, sorry I'm a few weeks late. Caught flu down in London."

Flu! Such a simple explanation, yet something like that hadn't even occurred to her. She felt the deep disappointment easing out of her, and pleasure at seeing him again taking over.

She also felt very guilty at doubting him. Of course, there was still the empty house to explain, but he was here, that was the important thing.

"You're fit again now, are you?" she asked anxiously.

"Fine, thanks, Grace."

She heaved a sigh of relief, but then he asked the inevitable question. "The record-player — did you find one for me?"

Grace glanced over to where the young lad was still examining the thing.

"I'm sorry, Leonard," she said. "It's down there. We couldn't keep it any longer."

She could see he was disappointed as he moved over and crouched down beside the boy. Well, she was disappointed, too, but what else could she have done?

She watched the grey head next to the fair, young one. They were talking about the player now, joking and chatting like a couple of boys with a new toy.

ABSENT-mindedly, Grace served other customers, wrong-changing one lady and dropping the other one's money on the floor.

Then, as she stood up after retrieving it, she heard the young lad say, "Well, I think I'll leave it to you, mate — nice, old job, though."

He ambled out of the shop, waving at Grace as he did so.

She was aware that Leonard was lifting the player and bringing it to the counter.

"I'll certainly take it then, Grace," he said, handing over the money. "Fit into my little flat nicely."

"Flat?" she queried.

"Yes, the house was too big for me now I'm alone. I moved before I went down to London. It hasn't sold yet, though, I'm afraid."

She handed him his change which he pocketed, and with two hands under the box, made towards the door, which someone opened for him.

Feeling miserable again, Grace watched him walk past the window. His search was over. Probably he wouldn't come back into the shop any more.

He was just a customer who had found what he wanted, wasn't he? But Grace knew there was more to it than that. There was for her, anyway.

They had seemed so easy together, more like old friends, than customer and assistant.

Presumably it must have been wishful thinking on her part, because he'd gone — no goodbye, not even a thank you.

The shop was empty now and Grace went to the room at the back. She needed a cup of tea.

Oh, bother! There was the door again. Unwillingly, she moved back into the shop.

"Grace." Leonard's smile was as warm as ever. "I wish you would come round this evening and listen to that record with me!"

"I'd like to do that, Leonard," Grace said. □

IT was half-way through the afternoon, my first, and already I was wondering if it hadn't been a terrible mistake. My arms were aching and my back — oh, my poor back!

Still, when your body hurts from head to toe, it concentrates the mind quite powerfully and takes it off your broken heart. That was the theory, anyway.

I'd done a lot of theorising recently, especially about this holiday. I mean, the last thing that I reckoned I should do was spend a fortnight lying on a sunny beach somewhere surrounded by marauding Romeos.

I'd had enough of men, and the prospect of long hours of idleness was daunting. It would only end in brooding days and tearful nights.

Best thing for me right then was some activity, one that would absorb me mentally and tire me physically. Best thing was simply to go off and work the memory of Robert and my failed engagement out of my system.

But as a volunteer on an excavation? Maybe, I reflected, thinking loving thoughts of sitting in the shadows with a long, cool drink, maybe it was a bit ambitious for someone whose nearest brush with exercise all year was changing ribbons on the typewriter.

It's not as if ideas of archaeology had ever interested me. In fact, they'd never even crossed my mind until I saw an advert for the project.

Full board and lodging were provided in return for services. No luxury and no nightlife, the leaflet I'd sent for said, but then I wasn't in the mood for those. I'd have them later, when my emotions were restored to normal. In the comfort of my flat, the project couldn't have seemed better.

A Future From The Past

It wasn't so idyllic in the blistering, August sun — not when I ached so fiercely in muscles whose mere existence came as an unpleasant shock, not when I had spent hours gazing at a stretch of barren earth. In my innocence, I'd expected to be digging treasure trove in every trowelful, but so far I hadn't found so much as an abandoned toffee paper.

I sighed and took a moment's breather, glancing at the man beside me.

by OLWEN RICHARDS

He was elderly, like all the others round me, and the sweat was trickling down his forehead as he worked. Beside him, tidily rolled up, his Fair Isle cardigan lay with a vacuum flask. Wise man to have come well-prepared for sudden chills or sudden thirsts. He must be an old hand at this excavating lark.

Five minutes more, I told myself, then I'd go and find the kitchen of the manor house. It couldn't be too far away, as we were digging in what had been the vegetable garden.

It was a lovely house, but the developers were moving in the following year. There would be chalets built in the grounds for tourists and if, as rumour had it, there'd been a Roman villa here, it would be lost for ever.

I bent again and scraped some soil aside half-heartedly.

THERE was a sudden, chinking noise. I stopped and stared excitedly.

"Oh, look!" I shouted to my neighbour. "I think I've found something."

He moved beside me, gazing where I pointed, then he bent and gently swept the area with his wrinkled hand.

"Looks like a fragment of mosaic."

"You think so?"

He nodded. "I'd say so, but I'm no expert. We'd better call the boss."

"I've only just arrived this morning and I don't know who he is," I answered, glancing round me vaguely.

"He's over there. I'll fetch him, if you like."

"I'd be most grateful, Mr . . ."

"Watkins. Alfred Watkins."

"Kate Marchant," I replied.

We shook hands solemnly, then laughed at the absurdity of being formal when we looked so casually dirty.

"Well, I suggest that you stand guard, Miss Marchant," my new friend advised. "You don't want to find that someone else has claimed your little triumph for their own."

I watched him as he approached another man. His back was to me, but I saw he wore a Fair Isle pullover.

I giggled. Somewhere, in the orchard underneath the apple trees, maybe, there must be such a cosy cache of patient wives knitting frenziedly, as much devoted to their patterning as all their menfolk were to digging!

I was on my knees again examining my treasure when the men returned.

"This is the Prof," Mr Watkins said.

I glanced up. What a shock I got! I'd no idea professors were so young. He wasn't more than 30, and he didn't fit my picture of a dried-up academic either.

He was really quite impressive with his shock of dark hair and his clear, blue eyes set off by sun-tanned skin.

"Professor Peter Watkins. He's my son," the old man added proudly.

I managed to suppress a smile. Perhaps there was just one poor, patient knitter sitting in an empty garden on her own . . .

I waited anxiously.

"Yes," Peter Watkins said at last. "It's genuine mosaic. The question now is how much we've got and whether we can save it."

I grabbed my trowel but his hand restrained me.

"No!" he said abruptly. "One touch and you could ruin it."

He ran his fingers through his hair abstractedly.

"These amateurs are lethal," he muttered to himself. Then, turning to me, he added, "Please leave the area alone. It's for the experts now."

How nice, I thought sarcastically. He could have been a little more polite. Requests are always preferable to orders and, besides, I felt some thanks were called for. I *was* an amateur, I knew, but I *had* discovered something valuable.

I left him to his feverish brushing, and walked slowly back towards the manor house. My faith in men, admittedly not strong since Robert left me, had taken yet another knock. Bath, food and bed were more important now.

I TOOK my simple soup and salad supper to a quiet table and sat down to read the local newspaper. It looked extremely boring, but I'd barely read the headline on the front page when my peace was interrupted.

"I wonder if you'd mind," a man's voice said. "If no-one's sitting here . . . The dining-room's so full tonight."

I smiled. It was the other Mr Watkins, looking cooler now and spruce. He introduced me to his wife and I suppressed a smile. I should have known her by the knitting-bag!

She was every bit as sweet as he was and modest, too. When I admired her husband's sweater she turned a little pink.

"It keeps me out of mischief, dear. I'm not a digger, I'm afraid, but I do so hate to stay behind. Besides, this way I never lose my menfolk in the crowd. Each sweater's an original. No two patterns are ever quite the same."

"That one's superb," I murmured.

"I based it on a fragment of a vase that Peter gave me," she replied. "I'm rather fond of it."

"It must be nice to have a clever son," I said, though privately I added that it would be nicer to have one possessed of good manners, too!

Peter Watkins joined us shortly afterwards and sat in silence, toying with his food and glancing at me now and then.

I wondered what was going through his mind — something unflattering about us amateurs, no doubt!

When his mother mentioned the mosaic, however, he began to talk — politely, unstoppably, and all fascinating stuff.

Despite myself, I warmed a little to a man so obviously passionate about his work, but when his parents said goodnight and left the two of us alone, my wariness returned.

There was a pub nearby, he said, charming, quaint, unmodernised. Perhaps I'd like to see it?

I declined, half out of genuine exhaustion, and half because I wasn't sure he wouldn't mock me again for my ham-fisted efforts.

All men might not be Roberts, I reflected, as I drifted into aching sleep, but why take chances?

Of course there's not much you can do if those same chances should take you — and they did!

It seemed I couldn't get away from Peter Watkins. He breakfasted with me next morning — quietly.

I put it down to my refusal of his offer of a drink, but suddenly he turned his blue eyes solemnly on me and reddened slightly.

"I feel I must apologise for yesterday. I shouldn't have said what I did about your wanting to dig farther. It was extremely rude."

I shrugged.

"It's just that I get so desperately involved in what I'm doing. The only thing that I can think of is preserving anything we find, not realising in the panic that I might be hurtful," he continued.

"I understand," I said, half-smiling at this unexpected honesty. "It would have been a tragedy if one careless blow from me had ruined what the centuries had left untouched."

"Perhaps you'd like to help me then? I've had another, closer look this morning, and I reckon that it's going to turn into a major find."

"I'd love to. But only if you show me what to do."

IT was a major find all right, the villa floor, so Peter thought. They were unearthing yet more stretches two weeks later when I left.

"You must come up again. It doesn't look much now, but when we've cleaned it up, you'll be amazed," he told me as he drove me to the station. "In fact, I'll get a section done this week, if you could get away on Friday."

"That's very quick." I smiled.

"It will be long enough without you, Kate," he murmured, so quietly I wasn't really sure he'd said it.

Still, if he did, I know he'll ring me in a day or so. Till then I've got the scarf his mother made me. She took the motif from the patch of the mosaic that they've called Kate's Corner, and she must have sat up nights to finish it in time.

I've got the other artefacts that turned up when we excavated farther. Peter made a present of them, as a memento, so he said, although my clearest memory is of the gentle pressure of his hand on mine as he was giving me an almost perfect dinner-plate and mug.

A pity that they're only mass-produced around 1965! But everyone's got to start somewhere!

It's funny, all the same, to think that my entire future looks like starting from a fragment of the past. □

Leave It To Gran!

by MARIAN HIPWELL

ELLEN'S heart sank as she caught sight of the figure making its way up the garden path. Not that she wasn't pleased to see her granddaughter, but judging from the way Kim was scowling, it looked as if Ellen was about to play peacemaker in yet another confrontation between mother and daughter.

"I've had it up to here with Mum!" Kim confirmed her fears as soon as she opened the door to her. "Honestly, Gran, I can't do anything right for her! If she's not nagging at me for one thing, she's at me for another —"

"Now let's calm down a bit." Ellen wasn't prepared to listen to criticism of Lorna. "Sit yourself down. I've got some of that squash in the fridge that you like so much.

"It isn't easy for your mum, you know," she added, turning towards the kitchen. "With the three of you to look after and your dad away —"

"*You* managed!" Kim pointed out swiftly. "And you had six!"

That was true, Ellen acknowledged. Their teens had been turbulent times, when she considered the well-balanced adults they were now.

Kim followed her into the kitchen, poking at this and that, helping herself to one of Ellen's freshly-baked biscuits without so much as a please or thank you.

Ellen eyed her granddaughter covertly as she found a glass and filled it with fruit juice. She loved her wholeheartedly, yet it was difficult at times to see the loving child she had once been in the rebellious young woman she was now.

That other person was in there somewhere, Ellen knew, and would come out again, when the time was right. But waiting for that glorious day could, at times, tax her patience a little . . .

"SO what was it this time?" Ellen asked briskly, handing Kim the drink.

"Same as always," Kim muttered. "Nagging at me to get up, do my homework, pick my clothes up, keep my room tidy. What doesn't she nag me about?

"Then she's forever on at me to eat my greens — ugh! She will insist on cooking all that stuff, when all I really want is fish fingers. And those puddings she makes! All that stodge!" She shuddered eloquently.

"She insists on my being home by ten o'clock, too. Ten o'clock! Then there's Jack." Her voice took on an injured tone. "She tries to hide it, but I know she can't stand the sight of him!"

"Jack?" Ellen queried.

"My new boyfriend," Kim explained. "Just because she doesn't like the way he looks —"

"Long hair?"

"Gran! Long hair went out yonks ago!" Kim regarded her with fond scorn. "It's all skin-heads now."

"Oh." Ellen accepted the rebuke meekly. "Well, I wouldn't know that, would I, dear?"

"Anyway," Kim took up her story again, "we had the worst row yet!" Her eyes smouldered. "Mum just doesn't understand me, Gran."

"And I do?" Ellen murmured.

"Of course you do!" Kim exclaimed. "Dad put his finger on it when he said you've got an understanding heart."

Ellen frowned. If she had an understanding heart, it was going to be working overtime on this occasion, to smooth things over between her daughter and her granddaughter.

It wasn't the first time she had been called on to pour oil on troubled waters. Lorna and Kim were too much alike — that was part of the trouble. Lorna had not been particularly rebellious in her teens, either, which made it difficult for her to understand her own daughter now.

Kim's tone took on a sulky tone. "I'm leaving home."

Ellen raised her eyebrows. Things were worse than she had realised.

"Where will you go?" she asked.

Kim looked defiant. "I don't know — perhaps to a friend. I'm definitely not going back."

Ellen frowned. Lorna, she knew, had tried every reasonable way to reach her daughter. *Every reasonable way,* she repeated to herself thoughtfully.

"What about staying here for a while?" she suggested. "A cooling-off period will be good for both of you."

"I hoped you'd say that." Kim looked relieved. "I'd be all right here. You won't nag and moan at me like Mum does. You understand me."

Ellen smiled. "Go and get your things, dear," she told her. "I'll give your mother a ring and explain."

FISH FINGERS! Great!" Kim came running into the kitchen later at Ellen's call and regarded the table enthusiastically.

"It's probably steak and cabbage at home." She pulled a face.

"Well, you're here now!" Ellen said briskly. "So eat up, dear.

"I didn't make a pudding, since you're so against them," she added apologetically.

"Oh, that's all right." Kim hesitated. "It's not all puddings I hate, Gran. Not that lovely meringue pie you used to make when we came to tea, or that chocolate sponge of yours. It melts in the mouth."

"We'll see," Ellen murmured. "I just didn't want to give you the same reasons for complaint that you had at home. You've come here to get away from nagging, after all, haven't you?"

"As if you would." Kim hugged her. "All right if I go out now? I've arranged to meet Jack."

"Of course it is," Ellen told her.

Despite her good intentions, Ellen had to bite her tongue firmly when Kim came down in jeans and blouse later. It wasn't that Ellen disapproved of jeans. It was the holes in the knees which drew her gaze, and the blouse appeared to be at least three sizes too large.

Catching her eye, Kim grinned.

"It's fashionable, Gran," she told her.

★   ★   ★   ★

"You haven't waited up for me, I hope?" Kim eyed her pensively when she returned around eleven o'clock that night, to find Ellen sitting reading.

"Of course not! I never go to bed before this time," Ellen assured her. "Enjoyed yourself?"

"Great!" Kim said enthusiastically.

Ellen waited, but the girl didn't elaborate.

"I'd love to meet Jack," Ellen ventured after a moment. "Please don't think he's not welcome here, whatever the situation at home. Bring him in next time he comes."

"All right." Kim didn't sound keen. "Goodnight, Gran."

"Goodnight, dear," Ellen murmured.

So ends the first day, she thought, as she locked up and made her way to bed. Let's see what tomorrow brings . . .

Tomorrow brought a distinctly annoyed Kim downstairs at nine-thirty.

"Gran!" She eyed Ellen reproachfully. "Why didn't you call me for school? I've an exam at ten o'clock!"

"But you said you hated being nagged to get up!" Ellen protested mildly.

"How did you get on?" she asked as her granddaughter walked into the house later that afternoon.

Kim put down her books with a decided thump.

"I got into trouble for not doing my homework," she muttered. "I forgot all about it. And I don't think I did too well in the exam."

"Never mind," Ellen said consolingly. "Come and have tea."

Kim's expression brightened when Ellen placed her food in front of her, then fell again when she saw the plate Ellen was taking from the oven.

Catching her glance, Ellen looked apologetic.

"It's only roast potatoes, carrots and steak, Kim," she told the girl. "I only made enough for myself, with you saying you hated that sort of thing.

Glorious Gardens
The Royal Palace of Falkland, Fife

FALKLAND PALACE was built in the 16th century as the country residence of the Stuart kings. The gardens, though, have a much more recent history, having been largely planned and planted since the Second World War.

Their main feature are the herbaceous borders, which form a magnificent foreground to the palace and Lomond Hills beyond. The colours of the Scottish Lion Rampant are echoed in the "August border," resplendent in yellow and red.

Leave It To Gran!

"That's all right." Kim's tone was noticeably lacking in enthusiasm. "I love fish fingers, Gran, I told you."

Yet the way she toyed with them had Ellen thinking she could be forgiven for doubting the fact.

"Gran! I can't find that blouse I left for washing!" Kim appeared at the top of the stairs later that evening.

Ellen, ironing in the kitchen, took her time about replying.

"Was it a green one?" she asked at last.

"That's right," Kim answered. "Have you seen it?"

"There's something green hanging over the radiator in the bathroom," Ellen told her. "That might be it. I didn't move it because I thought you might have left it there for some particular reason."

"I meant it to go in the wash." Kim sounded sheepish. "I wanted to wear it tonight."

"Oh dear." Ellen thought for a moment.

"Never mind," she said brightly then. "Put it in the wash now and it'll be done next time."

SOME time later, Kim came downstairs.

"Going out?" Ellen looked up over her glasses.

"Yes." Kim hesitated. "I've done my homework," she added.

"Good." Ellen's tone was gentle. "Jack coming for you?"

"Yes. That's probably him." Kim was moving towards the door in answer to a piercing whistle from the direction of the gate.

"Oh, bring him in, do!" Ellen was on her feet, moving to the door with her. "I can't have you thinking your friends aren't welcome here."

As Kim hesitated, Ellen opened the door and glanced towards the gate, beckoning as she saw a figure lingering there.

"It's Jack, isn't it?" she called. "Come on in and say hello."

"Gran —" Kim was eyeing her uneasily.

"Only for a moment, dear," Ellen spoke soothingly, "just so we can get to know each other."

She had steeled herself for her first sight of Jack, recalling Lorna's description of him. Her smile didn't waver as she took in the earring nestling close to the practically bald head, the shirt whose colours put Joseph's technicolour dream coat in the shade, and the jeans which made Kim's look the height of respectability.

"So you're Jack." She smiled at him. "I've heard a lot about you. Come on in."

She forestalled any protests by taking his arm and drawing him towards a chair.

Determinedly, she ignored the agonised expression on her granddaughter's face. She'd said she would welcome Kim's friends and that's just what she was doing, wasn't it?

The boy eyed Kim helplessly, then mumbled something which sounded to Ellen to be in a foreign language.

"And what sort of music are you into?" Ellen settled herself beside him, obviously preparing for a long chat. "I understand heavy metal's out these days. It's all rap now, isn't it? You strike me as being a rap fan."

She eyed him thoughtfully. "If you want to bring some records over, feel free to do so at any time. I love having young people about me. Isn't that right, Kim?"

The girl's face registered horror.

"We have to go, Gran," she said hastily.

Jack needed no second urging. He was on his feet in seconds.

"Well, if you must." Ellen spoke regretfully. "Sorry it's been so short this time, Jack. You must come to tea soon."

Jack gave her one last startled glance, then hurried after Kim.

Nothing further was said about the incident when Kim returned around eleven-fifteen, though her manner was somewhat subdued.

Ellen was in her dressing-gown, drinking cocoa.

"Oh, there you are!" She smiled, as Kim shut the door. "Good. I was just about to go to bed.

"I like Jack, by the way. He looks a most, er, unusual boy. Did he have anything to say about me after you left?"

"A bit," Kim muttered.

Ellen waited for her to elaborate, but there was nothing further. She had a feeling, though, that despite his apparently limited vocabulary, he'd had more than enough to say on the subject.

KIM was already up when Ellen came downstairs the following morning.

"I must dash — we've another examination and I don't want to be late. 'Bye."

"Oh, by the way —" She stopped, eyeing Ellen uncertainly. "I put that blouse in the washing-basket, and some other things. Will you be doing any washing today?"

"I expect I will," Ellen said.

There was a little smile playing about her mouth as she went to put the kettle on, and it wasn't at the prospect of a cup of tea . . .

Kim's eyes brightened as she caught the smell wafting from the grill when she came home later that day.

"Beefburgers — great!" she said.

"Thought it might make a change." Ellen looked up from the bread she had been buttering.

"I made a pudding, too," she went on half-apologetically, indicating the sponge she had just taken out of the oven. "But remembering what you said about stodge, I don't imagine you'll be wanting any —"

"Well, just this once," Kim cut in swiftly, her eyes lingering on the sponge.

The girl's appetite seemed to be improving as the week wore on . . .

"Off out again?" she queried as Kim came downstairs around seven o'clock, dressed to go out.

"Yes. Thanks for washing and ironing the blouse, Gran."

Leave It To Gran!

"No trouble," Ellen said. "Is Jack coming for you?"

"No, he said he'd meet me in town." Kim gave Ellen an uneasy glance.

"Pity." Ellen suppressed a sigh. "I'd have enjoyed chatting with him again. Well, have a nice time, dear."

It had been a hard week in a lot of ways, she reflected, when Kim had gone. And the hardest part of all was closing and locking the inner front door firmly when Kim hadn't returned by eleven-thirty, pocketing the key and going upstairs to bed.

True, she had left the porch door unlocked for the girl, but it still went against everything in her. She hadn't expected to sleep, yet when the alarm she had set went off at three-thirty, she jumped, realising she had dozed off. Donning her dressing-gown, she went downstairs.

Kim was curled up in the porch, fast asleep, though she awoke quickly enough when Ellen shook her arm.

"What? Oh, Gran!" She eyed Ellen indignantly. "You locked me out!"

"I told you — I go to bed around eleven," Ellen informed her. "I got up for an aspirin. I've got a headache. You surely wouldn't want me waiting up for you, after all you said about your mother doing that?"

"But you didn't have to lock the door, surely?" Kim complained.

"What?" Ellen asked. "Leave the door open in this day and age? There have been two burglaries already on this road!"

THE following evening, Kim was home before ten o'clock. The evening after that, she didn't go out at all. She even offered to do the ironing which Ellen had left for the morning.

Ellen eyed her granddaughter as she worked. The iron was flying over the cloth and she was humming along with the television music. It was, Ellen noted, the first time that week she had seen Kim without that sulky twist to her mouth.

It didn't surprise her when, on Saturday morning, Kim thanked her very much for having her and told her she was thinking of going home.

Ellen didn't probe. She had a feeling, somehow, that the less said between them just now, the better.

Later, she telephoned Lorna to let her know Kim was on her way. They chatted for a few moments.

"I think you might find things a little better between the two of you now," Ellen said. "I hope so, anyway.

"And Lorna —" She hesitated. "If anything Kim says leads you to feel that I might, perhaps, have acted, shall we say a little *unreasonably* whilst she was here, you do realise, don't you, that it's only because I love her?"

She listened for a moment, then nodded. "Yes, I expect you're right about that, dear. I've been told before that I have an understanding heart . . ." □

HOP down then, lass, and put your clothes on."
The doctor rattled shut the cubicle curtains.

Catriona dressed slowly, shaking.

But Dr Barr had a reassuring smile. "Good news, Mrs Gregg. I find nothing wrong, physically."

There was a moment's pause. "But —"

Catriona's heart raced again.

"I think you could do with a break, a week away from the children. It's hard work bringing up a family, and you're a specially devoted mum, I know that.

"Try a break away if you can — make it a second honeymoon, just you and your husband."

Just you and your husband.

Catriona Gregg stopped listening at this point. Her kind doctor was getting it all wrong.

Wasn't it her relationship these days with Duncan which had driven her to see the doctor, to check if maybe some virus was causing the nightmare fear that their 10-year-old marriage was heading perilously close to the rocks!

She walked home through the rush-hour streets. Why take a bus? Why hurry home to a husband immersed in the evening paper, or crouched over scattered business files at the table?

Catriona stared as she passed shop windows, not seeing the bright displays, her mind's eye caught up only with looking back — back 10 years . . .

THERE had been the fantastic wedding, on a day filled with sunshine. Then there was the the honeymoon hotel by the edge of the sea on Skye.

Catriona Gregg saw again, as if unrolled on a tiny film-screen, Duncan and herself walking hand hand in hand on their last day along the rocky shore. A fierce downpour sent them hurrying for shelter.

Among the dark shadows and haunting echoes of a cave, they scoffed their packed lunch and shared the half-bottle of champagne (compliments of the sentimental manager of the honeymoon hotel!).

It was Duncan's idea that they should place a message inside the empty bottle and hide it in the cave, which surely proved beyond all

by LAURA CALDWELL

MAGIC

doubt, Catriona decided unhappily now, what a daft, romantic guy her husband was — correction, *had been.*

Her young husband wrote on a scrap of paper torn from his diary: *Catriona, I promise my love will stay fresh and true till the seas round Skye run dry. Duncan Gregg.*

She added: *Me, too. Love you always and for ever.*

Together, solemn as a pair of church mice, they sealed the bottle with a strip of sticking plaster and hid it in a deep hollow behind some stones.

"We'll come back every summer to check it's safe," Duncan vowed.

As things turned out, 10 years on with three children and Duncan's redundancy, the Greggs had never managed back to Skye. The enchanted island was a long trip from Newcastle. Catriona was for ever occupied looking after Alan and Karen and Tommy. Duncan, this past year, had been working like a beaver to build up his own, small, textile business. There just had never been time or spare cash for such a holiday.

But the young couple didn't forget the romantic, honeymoon episode. They talked about it often, and their love for each other had stayed fresh and true.

Then one day the talking stopped — not just talking about Skye, talking about *anything*, not communicating.

WALKING home, Catriona thought, Duncan's changed. He isn't listening when I tell him about my day, about the children and their teachers and chums, their colds, coughs and tummy upsets, visits to the dentist and school reports!

He's become like an ostrich, his head buried in his work. He's forgotten the promise hidden in the island cave.

As for the idea of her reminding him, Catriona knew, she just *knew*, her husband's reaction would be to hide, red-faced, behind his newspaper! Or worse, far worse, maybe he'd *laugh.*

Saturday would be their tenth anniversary. Catriona had already baked a cake, fixed 10 candles, piped a pretty chocolate heart. She would make a special meal, with peppered steak (Duncan's favourite). She had some crackers and balloons left over from Christmas.

If Duncan hadn't remembered the special day — no, oh no, Catriona couldn't face that! Nor would she remind him . . .

Her husband was alone when she reached home, the boys at Cubs, Karen invited to tea next door.

"How did it go? All right?" He looked anxious.

What was Duncan talking about? For a wild moment Catriona thought he must guess about the unhappy turmoil in her mind. But, of course, he was only asking about her visit to Dr Barr. "All right. He says I'm a bit tired, that's all."

"Aren't we all! I'll make you a cup of tea." But he had no tender smile. Worse, there was no mention that Saturday was their special day!

Later, avoiding her eyes, Duncan said, "I have to go away tomorrow and I'll be away overnight. There's a chance of a contract in Aberdeen I daren't miss. I'll be home late on Saturday."

★   ★   ★   ★

It was half-an-hour from midnight when Duncan did at last arrive home.

"I'll heat up some dinner for you."

"Don't bother. I stopped on the way down."

He had actually used some precious time to have a meal, she thought!

Next came the bombshell. "We must talk, Catriona. I haven't been near Aberdeen . . ."

Her heart bleak, Catriona braced herself to hear the truth.

"These past months I've been thinking a lot about us, about our marriage." His voice was solemn. "We'd nothing real to say to each other any more. Something had gone, and so —"

She steeled herself to listen. "And so when it came close to our anniversary and you never once mentioned it . . .

"I just felt like digging my heels in. Stupidly I decided I wouldn't be the one to remind you!"

Catriona thought, this is incredible! Duncan's fears were turning out to be identical to her own!

"But I was desperately unhappy, Catriona. We'd lost sight of something precious. I knew I had to find it and bring it back.

"I didn't head for Aberdeen — that was a wee white lie. I found myself at Kyle of Lochalsh getting on to the Skye ferry."

Now Duncan Gregg was reaching into his pocket, triumphantly holding up the 10-year-old champagne bottle. "It was there, safe and snug in the cave just as we'd left it.

"The seas round Skye hadn't run dry after all, though yesterday they were stormy. And I thought maybe they were a wee bit like our marriage, Catriona, needing a shot of sunshine and blue skies!"

Then Duncan took her in his arms.

LATER they made coffee, and Catriona brought out her beautiful cake. The fresh love they'd nearly lost flowed over them.

It seemed Duncan wasn't finished yet. "There's something else I've to tell you." He crunched happily into the chocolate heart. "This champagne bottle must be returned to its island hide-away pronto.

"It's all fixed, sweetheart. I stopped off in Glasgow on my way home tonight to have a talk with Gran and Grandpa. It appears they're longing to come to look after their grandchildren. They're arriving the day before we take off for Skye — just the two of us.

"It's what we've both been needing for a long time — a second honeymoon! Right?"

It was just what the doctor ordered. What a nice, daft, romantic guy Duncan Gregg had always been! □

PLEA FROM THE HEART

I VY stopped in front of the hall
mirror to tuck her scarf into
her best coat. She settled her
felt hat on her grey hair, pushing a
hatpin through her bun.

She must look her best for
tonight's meeting at the village
hall. A council representative was
coming and he had to be made to
realise these were no country
bumpkins he was dealing with.

"Gipsies!" She snorted at her
reflection. "In Turner's field!"

Admittedly, it was too boggy for
farming, and it had stood six foot
high in weeds for many a year.
But that was no excuse for making
a caravan camp for tinkers.

The village was united on that,
because all the houses overlooked
Turner's field. The only dissenter
had been Adams at the Dog and
Pheasant — he saw profit on the
horizon. His wife had sorted him
out, saying his regulars would
defect to the Red Lion in the next
village at the first sign of a gipsy
in the bar. A petition form
immediately appeared on the
counter.

It had done no good. The
council seemed determined to go
ahead.

But the villagers weren't beaten.
Tonight they'd enlisted the help of
a local bank clerk who'd once
spent six months in a solicitor's
office in London, and reckoned he
could run legal rings round any
council chap.

Not that anyone had much faith
in him. Their real hope lay in the
lady botanist who was to speak of
Turner's field as the site of many
rare and endangered species. To
the locals they looked like any
other old weeds, but they'd back
her to the hilt if it would stop the
gipsy invasion.

Ivy, hoping to invite her for
supper, made a mental check of the
preparations. Chicken salad in the
fridge, plates of sandwiches and
cakes in Clingfilm on the kitchen
table, China tea as well as Indian,
and coffee.

by HELEN McKENZIE

She smiled at her reflection. Perfect!

It was nearly five o'clock. The meeting wasn't till seven, but she wanted to post a letter and still be early enough to get a seat at the front, in case she found the courage to speak herself.

HALFWAY down the garden path, something small and hard cannoned into her, stopping her, breathless, in her tracks.

Ivy looked down. A small girl was clinging to her coat, the chill October wind blowing strands of dirty blonde hair across her tear-stained face. She was painfully thin and shivering in a cotton dress.

"Please, Miss. Come quick. It's my ma. She's bad, real bad, Miss."

"What?" Ivy said. "Where?"

"In our van, Miss, by the river. Oh, do come, Miss."

The child tugged at her coat and began to run, pulling Ivy after her.

"We'll have to go slower," Ivy panted. "I'm too old to run."

She stopped for breath, pulling off her scarf and wrapping it round the child's shoulders.

"What's your name?" she asked as they started again at a trot.

"Hann, Miss. Oh, do hurry, Miss. She's ever so sick."

"Did you leave her alone?"

"No, Miss. Jos stayed."

"Jos?"

"My little sister. She's only five and she's ever so scared. *I'm* seven," she added proudly. "And a half."

Ivy tried to move faster despite the ache developing in her legs. A sick woman needed more than a five-year-old to look after her.

Hann's mother lay on a narrow bunk, her face grey with pain. She clutched her stomach and moaned now and then.

Jos, who was trying to keep her covered with a ragged blanket, got up and ran to Hann for comfort.

"She's been awful sick, Hann," she sobbed, pointing to a bowl on the floor.

"We'll need a doctor, Hann," Ivy said. "Will you be all right while I go home and ring?"

"Yes, Miss."

Ivy and stroked the woman's forehead gently.

"It's all right," she murmured. "We'll soon have you looked after."

ETERNITY passed before the doctor arrived with an ambulance. The men stretchered Hann's mother off across the marshy ground.

"Just in time, I reckon," the doctor remarked as he watched them pull away. "Acute appendicitis. Wouldn't have lasted much longer."

The children clung to Ivy, wide-eyed with fear.

"Now," he said, "these two can't stay here long."

He looked at Hann. "Where's your father, young lady?"

"Dunno." Hann's voice was hostile.

"When'll he be back?" Ivy's was gentler, and Hann relaxed.

"Dunno, Miss. He went off months ago. All drunk he was, Miss. Hit our ma, then got in the van and went. Never seen him since. Never want to, neither."

"I'll ring the Social Services and find a short-stay home," the doctor decided.

The children shrank behind Ivy.

"Don't let him put us away, Miss," Hann pleaded, clutching the sobbing Jos.

Ivy thought for a moment.

"Look," she said, "it's getting late. Let me have them, for tonight, at least. We'll sort things out tomorrow."

The doctor looked doubtful. "Can you cope?"

"I'll manage."

She turned to the children. "Would you like to come and stay with me?"

"Oh yes, Miss," they chorused.

"Please," Hann added, nudging her sister.

"Please," Jos repeated obediently, and Ivy smiled. They reminded her of her own grandchildren "learning manners."

Thanks to those two, she kept the spare beds ready for sudden visits, and pyjamas clean and waiting in a drawer.

Her only dilemma was whether to clean Hann and Jos first or feed them.

"Have you eaten?" she asked.

Hann nodded. "Yes, Miss. Bread and jam at dinner-time."

Ivy frowned. "In that case you must be starving."

Ivy led the way into the kitchen and scrubbed their hands at the sink. The rest of the dirt could wait.

The children's eyes grew large at the sight of the sandwiches and then larger still . . .

"What's that?" Jos whispered.

"Chicken," Hann replied. "Smashing. We had one once when you were this big." She cradled her arms and made a rocking movement.

"Our dad fetched one home," she explained to Ivy. "It had all its feathers on. Still warm, it was, from being caught."

She watched Ivy cutting long, thin slices.

"Mostly we have stew," she confided. "Veg and that. Whatever we can pinch from the fields. Sometimes our dad got a rabbit or a pigeon.

"And sometimes —" she paused for effect "— we had beans. Proper beans, from a tin."

Despite her smile, Ivy's heart ached for them.

L ATER Ivy took the children upstairs.
Hann submitted stoically to having her hair washed, then sat hunched miserably in the warm bath.

But Jos screamed throughout, sobbing violently when set beside her sister in the unfamiliar water.

Ivy was racking her brains for some way of reconciling them to the experience, when Hann suddenly took a handful of bubbles and blew them at Jos . . .

They looked different children already as Ivy bent to kiss them goodnight.

Hann flung her arms round Ivy's neck and kissed back.

"Thank you, Miss," she whispered. "And make our ma well soon."

Ivy lay awake, staring into the darkness, thinking of Turner's field. She was glad she hadn't been there to applaud the lady botanist, glad she hadn't joined the general protest.

"Gipsies," she said to herself sternly, "are people, too."

★　　　★　　　★　　　★

They arrived at the hospital clutching cuddly toys from Ivy's attic and handfuls of late-flowering weeds from Turner's field. Too weak to speak, their mother smiled faintly and lay, their hands clasped in hers.

Sister Watson looked at Ivy. "Mrs Vennor's through the operation OK, but she's very undernourished. We'll have to keep her in a while just to feed her up."

"Don't worry about the children," Ivy said. "I'll be only too happy . . ."

"But afterwards." Vera Watson's face was grim. "That van!"

"I've been thinking about that myself. When Tom sold off our farm he kept that bit of a field by the river. Said he couldn't sell our whole life together.

"I laughed at him then, but seems it might come in handy after all. There's that old cottage on it."

"Yes, but it's a bit tumbledown," Sister Watson pointed out doubtfully.

"Sound as a bell. Nothing a lick of paint and a bit of second-hand furniture wouldn't fix," Ivy said firmly.

AND fix it she did. By spring the cottage was unrecognisable. So were its inhabitants, all three rosy-cheeked and blooming.

Ivy had wheedled the doctor into taking Mrs Vennor on for a few hours a week to clean the surgery, and gradually other villagers had followed his example. The family's regular, if small, income was boosted when Adams grudgingly offered a few evenings' work in the bar.

Ivy baby-sat, rejoicing to see the outcasts accepted into the fabric of village life, with Hann and Jos settled into the school, making friends.

Turner's field remained a problem. The proposals had gone to a higher level, thanks to the evidence of the lady botanist and the volume of local protest. But there was a rumour that, if the weeds should win the day, there'd be a new petition in the bar.

People, as Adams himself said, smiling at his popular new barmaid, were people, after all, and needed protection. □

I KNOW A LAND WHERE CHILDREN GO...

I KNOW a land where children go,
  Once they've been tucked in bed,
A land that no-one else can find,
  For it lies within their head.

This is the land of wish-come-true,
  But all is not as it seems,
It's also the land of broken-heart,
  For this is the land of dreams.

This is where they swim the seas,
  Or scale the mountains high,
This is where they roam the plains,
  Or glide across the sky.

Here they can be a buccaneer,
  Or a knight upon his steed,
Perhaps they'll find a sunken ship,
  Or help a friend in need.

But sometimes in the land of dreams,
  They wish that they weren't there,
For fun can quickly turn to fear,
  And a dream become nightmare.

No matter how many times they go,
  It's never twice the same,
And though it seems so very real,
  Few memories will remain.

I know a land where children go,
  Once they've been tucked in bed,
A land that's theirs, and theirs alone,
  For it lies within their head.

— Joan Coatswith.

TIME TO THINK AGAIN

ANDY groaned as he put down the telephone. There was no way round it — he would have to go home at Christmas.

His secretary looked at him inquiringly.

"What's wrong?"

"You'll have to cancel my skiing trip, Judith. I'm sorry, but there's business at home I have to take care of. The only time that's mutually convenient to the solicitor and myself is between Christmas and New Year."

"I'm surprised the solicitor is opening his office. A lot of offices close down completely at the end of the year these days."

"As we do!" Andy agreed. "However, old man Johnstone is one of the old school. Christmas Day, Boxing Day and New Year's Day are allowed, otherwise it's business as usual."

"You never seem to go home at Christmas," Judith ventured awkwardly. "I know your parents have passed on now, but even when they were still alive you didn't go home for Christmas."

"Well, you know what they say," Andy said smiling. "Home is where the heart is, and I'm afraid mine isn't there — not since my sister married, anyway."

He spoke lightly, but, Judith thought, he really means it. He goes away each Christmas, because there's no-one for him to go home to. How awful!

She really looked forward to going back. She welcomed the chance of returning to the familiar faces, the certainty of her parents' affection and welcome, the security of their own, little, family traditions. Andy obviously had nothing like that to enjoy.

Judith couldn't help wondering

by
**LINDA
LEIGH**

whether I went back for the festive season or not.

"But the main reason is because I lost someone of whom I was very fond one Christmas Eve, and the memories were very painful for me. However, it all happened a long time ago."

Long time ago or not, Judith thought, the shadow is still with you. I wonder who she was! You must have loved her very much!

When she went to say goodbye on Christmas Eve, he kissed her warmly.

"'Happy Christmas and New Year, Judith. Have a good rest, you deserve it.''

f being amongst a crowd of holi-daymaking strangers mightn't make him feel even more isolated. How sad that being alone in a crowd was better than being alone with oneself!

S OMETHING must have shown in her face.

"It's all right, Judith," he said reassuringly. "Don't worry about it. I was never close to my parents as you are to yours, and t, didn't really bother them

"Thanks, Andy. I'm sorry you're missing out on your skiing this year. Nevertheless I hope somehow you have a Christmas like mine. I can't wish you more than that!"

"Peace on earth, goodwill towards men, eh?" he teased. "Thanks, Judith. That's very kind of you, and I do appreciate it. Now, let's lock up. I'll drop you at the station, and see you again next year."

He thought about Judith as he drove homewards. She was part of a family, just as Derry had been. She would never understand what it was like to be in a family, but not of it.

Even though he was a few years younger, Derry had recognised the difference between his family and Andy's. There were a mother and father, brother and sister in each, but in Derry's house there were love and interest and warmth between all the members. The only affection in Derry's life came from his sister.

Whose fault, he wondered? The father he couldn't remember who had been killed in a road accident when he was a few months old? His mother, who resented him as living proof of her indiscretion? His grandparents, who had insisted on the marriage of the two unwilling youngsters?

Would life have been different if his father had lived? He'd never know. All he did know was that his mother had married again, and although he had always been well-fed and clothed, he had always been aware that his mother and step-father did what they did only out of a sense of duty or obligation.

There had never had any real interest in or fondness for him. That had all gone to Deirdre, who had been born when he was three years old. As soon as he saw her, Andy had been captivated by his little sister, and she, luckily, adored him in return. If it hadn't been for Deirdre's wholehearted affection, his life would have been bleak indeed.

It was through Deirdre he met Derry. Derry was her first boyfriend, and Andy liked him immediately. A mutual interest in motor bikes cemented the friendship which grew steadily over the next couple of years.

It had been the happiest time of his life. As well as Deirdre he had Derry, too. He knew Judith had assumed he had been talking about a girlfriend, and he hadn't enlightened her, but it was Derry he had lost on that Christmas Eve years ago.

ANDY realised he'd reached his destination. The old place hadn't changed at all, he reflected. Actually, it wasn't so very old.

It was, in fact, a very nice bungalow. He let it out when he could, but hadn't put it up for sale in case Deirdre might want it.

Now she and her husband had decided to stay in Australia, there wasn't much point in hanging on to it. He certainly had no intention of ever living in it again.

He turned on the central heating, took in the groceries, had a hot bath as soon as the water was hot enough, then something to eat.

Once that was done he wandered around restlessly. Nothing

appealed to him on television. He couldn't concentrate on reading. The house was too empty.

If Deirdre were with him it would be different, but apart from those of her, all his memories were cold ones. It was no good, he could never settle here. He should have booked into a hotel.

Well, he was obliged to stay now until he saw old Johnstone on the 27th, and finalised the estate.

He'd go to church, he decided. Perhaps by the time the Watch Night Service was over, the day's work and long drive would have caught up with him and he'd be able to sleep.

He saw Derry's mother as she returned to her seat after taking communion. It came as a shock. It hadn't occurred to him he might see her.

He spoke to her after the service. "How are you, Mrs Westhead?"

Mrs Westhead turned and her eyes widened in surprise. "Andrew!"

"Are you keeping well?"

She was always polite, he had to admit that, but once her eyes had smiled at him when she saw him. Now they were expressionless. He didn't blame her, of course.

"Yes, thank you, Andrew. And you?"

"Yes, very well."

He wanted to say . . . What did he want to say? "I'm sorry. I know how you must miss him. I can't forget, either! Time dulls the pain, but it's still there, always will be."

The silence hung heavily between them.

"All the best, Andrew!"

He couldn't say, "Happy Christmas." Ten years ago at Christmastime he'd killed her son.

"All the best, Mrs Westhead."

NEXT morning after breakfast, Andy opened the presents from Deirdre and Judith. He had a headache, and as it was a crisp, clear morning he strolled into the garden for a breath of fresh air.

He saw them, nestling close to the ground, flowering in quiet beauty beside the yellow jasmine, just as they had done 10 years ago — Christmas roses.

The memories returned, sharp and clear.

Derry had asked if he could take some for his mother. "She loves Christmas roses. I don't know what's happened to ours, but they're all dead now."

"Take what you like. Put some winter flowering jasmine with them. They look nice together."

He remembered Mrs Westhead's pleasure when she was given the posy.

Almost before he had realised it, he had made up a bouquet of roses and jasmine and was in the car.

Mrs Westhead's surprise was undisguised.

"Andrew! What are you doing here?"
▶ *p108*

SANDSTONE ARCH, TORNESS, EAST LOTHIAN
J CAMPBELL KERR

"I saw these in the garden, and I remembered how much you liked them. I thought you might like to have them."

He saw the pain and sudden brightness of tears in her eyes. He knew she was remembering, as he had done, the posy she'd been given so long ago.

"Mrs Westhead, I don't mean to upset you, truly I don't. I just saw them, and thought how lovely they looked. Somehow it seemed important to share them with you. I'm sorry — I shouldn't have come."

Mrs Westhead pulled herself together. "It was a kind thought, Andrew."

At least she had taken the gesture in the right way. She wasn't going to accuse him of insensitivity and re-opening old wounds.

"Thank you." She smiled, but the smile didn't quite reach her eyes. "Would you care to come in and have a cup of coffee?"

She was asking because she was a polite lady, caught unawares, taking refuge in the formalities. Andy realised that.

She didn't really *want* to invite him inside, but Andy accepted. Perhaps he'd be able to talk about Derry, but what was there to say that hadn't been said already?

She was composed when she brought in the tray of coffee and mince pies.

"You don't usually come back for Christmas, do you, Andrew?"

He took the bull by the horns. "Never, since Derry died, except for a couple of occasions when I couldn't avoid it. I wouldn't be here now if it wasn't for having to clear up Mother's estate with the solicitor."

Mrs Westhead's lips tightened at the mention of her son, but she refused to be drawn.

"Yes, I saw your mother had died," was all she said. "Your business is doing well, is it?"

"Not as well as I'd like but I'm keeping my head above water, so I can't complain." Perhaps he was being perverse, but he was determined to re-open the subject of her family. "I wasn't sure you'd be

◄ p 107

SANDSTONE ARCH, TORNESS, EAST LOTHIAN

Rail travellers between Edinburgh and London have an opportunity of seeing attractive coastal scenery. Just south of Torness is an interesting geological formation where the very first "clash" between Scotland and England occurred 400 million years ago. The English rocks collided, in slow motion, with the Scottish rocks, something like a multiple crash on a motorway.

in. I thought you might spend Christmas Day with Sue and her family?"

Sue was Derry's sister.

"They've already been on the phone, and I'll spend Boxing Day with them, but I prefer to have Christmas Day on my own."

Andy knew Mr Westhead had had a fatal heart attack several years ago.

"Don't you mind being on your own?" he asked.

Her voice was harsh. "One gets used to it."

Used to it, but not resigned to it, Andy thought. He could understand that.

H E looked around the room appreciatively. It had changed very little. Mrs Westhead might live alone, but there was still a cheerful, welcoming aura everywhere.

"Do you remember how we used to play Monopoly in here?" he asked. "Mr Westland and Deirdre always seemed to win. You, Derry and I were never able to compete with them, though Sue sometimes did."

"Of course I remember." Mrs Westhead's tone was cool.

The unspoken reproof was there. *He* might forget, she never would!

"I don't think you ever knew how much I enjoyed coming here," Andy said. "It was so different from my own home."

"Different?"

"Yes, you were all so interested and involved with one another. You shared all your worries and successes. What happened to one member of the family was important to all. I envied you that."

"I don't understand, Andrew. Your parents looked after you very well, and saw you had a good education."

"Yes, they did indeed. They did everything expected of them," he agreed. "The only they didn't do was to take a genuine interest in me, to care what happened to me or how I felt.

"It wasn't until I came here that I discovered what a real family was like. Up till then I thought it more or less normal for parents to be indifferent to their sons."

"I'm sorry," Mrs Westhead said slowly. "I didn't know . . ."

"There was no reason why you should. Derry did, though. That was why he asked Deirdre and her big brother over so often. He knew how much I appreciated and enjoyed the interest you and Mr Westhead showed in us."

Mrs Westhead said nothing.

What was she thinking, Andy wondered. That he'd shown precious little gratitude for that interest, taking away their only son at 16 years of age?

"You still hold me responsible for Derry's death, don't you?"

"I've never blamed you, Andrew."

"Yes, you have, Mrs Westhead. You've never said so in words, but in your heart you've always thought it was my fault." Andy's voice was raw with emotion. "Well, you can't blame me any more than I blame myself."

"I *told* you it was dangerous. I *asked* you not to take him . . ." Mrs Westhead's voice was choked.

"I know! I know!" Andy said roughly.

They'd taken over the posy of flowers, then invited Derry's parents to look at the new motor-bike that was Andy's special Christmas present.

Derry had his photograph taken beside it, as though it belonged to him.

"I'd like one the same in a couple of years' time," he'd warned Mr and Mrs Westhead. "Andy's got to go and deliver a Christmas present for his parents. You don't mind if I gò with him, do you? We'll be back by eight o'clock."

Mrs Westhead had been unwilling. It would be dark when they were riding home, and the weathermen were forecasting icy roads.

"I'll be very careful," Andy had said. "I've been riding a motor-bike for eighteen months now. I know what I'm doing. I'll not take any chances, I promise."

"Please, Mum," Derry had pleaded, and in the end she'd given in.

Andy had been careful, very careful. He'd stopped at the road junction. He'd been stationary when the car with the driver who had already had too much to drink failed to brake in time, skidded on the frosty road and knocked them into the path of the oncoming traffic.

Nausea swept over him.

He stood up abruptly. "I shouldn't have come. I'm sorry. I didn't mean to bring back painful memories.

"But at least you *have* memories of all the years you and Mr Westhead had together, of the time you both had with Sue and Derry. And you still have Sue and her family to care for and care for you."

Andy's voice was bitter. "My memories are very restricted! I'd better go. Don't bother to see me out. Goodbye, Mrs Westhead. Thanks for the coffee."

Mrs Westhead made no move to stop him, and he left, regretting the impulse that had taken him there in the first place, to freshen in both their minds events neither of them could forget.

▶ *over*

BALMORAL CASTLE, GRAMPIAN

Purchased by the Prince Consort in 1852, who organised a programme of rebuilding, this is the Queen's Highland home. The castle is surrounded by a large estate providing excellent fishing, stalking and shooting and, importantly, privacy. The estate was first recorded in 1484 as "Bouchmorale."

BALMORAL CASTLE, GRAMPIAN : J CAMPBELL KERR

MRS WESTHEAD was trembling when she picked up the tray and carried it out to the kitchen. She wished he hadn't come. Why had she invited him ? Because Derry had been so fond of him, that was why.

But Derry was gone now. While other people celebrated the birth of a saviour, she mourned the death of a son.

At least you have memories, he'd said. How dare he! Memories were a poor substitute for the husband and son she still missed, and the son might still be here had it not been for Andrew and his motor-bike!

On her way back to the sitting room, still agitated, her eyes fell on the photograph on the sideboard, the last one ever taken of him. She picked it up and took it with her, studying it when she sat down, her eyes full of tears.

Derry was standing proudly by a motor-bike, his face alight with pleasure. Almost out of view in the background, leaning against the wall, watching with tolerant affection, was a 19-year-old youth.

How young they look, Mrs Westhead thought. With sudden, overwhelming clarity she remembered them setting off on that fateful ride, cheerfully waving goodbye, their young faces confident and untroubled.

She thought about the next time she had seen Andrew, after the accident. The boyishness had vanished from his face, never to return, and his eyes were haunted.

Andrew and Derry had been good friends, despite their three-year age difference. Andrew was bound to have been upset by what happened.

She had lost a son, but what had Andrew lost? More than a friend, judging from what he had just said, if not quite a brother. The Westheads had comforted one another, but had offered none to him. It had never occurred to her until this moment that Andrew's grief could be equal to their own.

Now she wondered if Andrew's could have been greater, knowing that Derry would have lived if he hadn't taken him on the pillion.

She acknowledged slowly that what Andrew had said was true. She did blame him for Derry's death. She had never said that to him or anyone else.

The logical part of her mind had accepted that he had taken every precaution. If they had set out five minutes earlier, if the other car had reached the junction two minutes later, the accident wouldn't have happened. As it was, it was the drunken driver to blame, not Andrew. Yet the emotional side of her *did* hold him responsible. Until today, she hadn't fully appreciated that deep down she had always felt it had been Andrew's fault, though she had concealed the resentment even from herself.

She remembered Andrew's remarks about his parents' indifference, their coldness. She had been just the same, hadn't she? She'd said Andrew wasn't to blame and not to reproach himself, without really meaning it.

She hadn't offered him any condolences or sympathy. Had anyone, apart from his sister? If not, he'd had a heavy load to bear these past 10 years.

SHE looked at the bouquet of Christmas roses. They were beautiful. Tears flooded her eyes once more. Her thoughts returned to Andrew, and his anguished expression when he left.

He was right, the Westheads had been a proper family — they had loved, laughed and cried together, and they did have memories.

But who had cried with Andrew, who had loved him? Had those two brief years of friendship with their family really meant so much to him? If so, he must indeed be a very lonely young man.

Her hands caressed the flowers. She knew he had meant well when he brought them to her. It had been kind of him to make the effort and come. Had it taken a lot of courage, too?

Words of a carol being sung on the radio caught her attention. "Peace on earth, goodwill to men . . ."

Perhaps the time was ripe for some active peace and goodwill on her part?

Derry's face smiled at her from the photograph.

She looked up the telephone number and dialled it.

"Andrew? It's Mrs Westhead. Do you think you could spare the time to come and see me again before you go? I've a photograph I think you might like to have. In fact, if you haven't any other plans, I'd be delighted if you'd return and have lunch with me."

★   ★   ★   ★

When Judith came into his office, she saw immediately that Andy was already at work in his, whistling cheerfully. He must have heard her arrive because he came to see her straight away.

"Good morning, Judith. Have you had a good holiday?"

"Yes, thank you." She turned to wish him a happy New Year then stared, puzzled.

There was something different about him, something she couldn't pin down, almost indefinable, but definitely there. He looked at ease, as though a load had been taken from him.

"Did you manage to sort everything out?" she asked.

"Yes, everything," he agreed.

"And you're definitely selling the house?"

"No, actually I've decided to let it at a nominal rent, to a lady I know. She lives on her own now and finds stairs are becoming a problem. A bungalow will be far better for her."

"I see," she said, though she didn't. "Well, I hope you had a happy Christmas even though you didn't get away."

"Yes, Judith," he said. "I did. I had one of your Christmasses."

"Mine?" She didn't understand for a moment. "Oh, a 'peace on earth, goodwill to men' sort of Christmas?"

He nodded. One day he might explain.

He held out a large posy of Christmas roses.

"Happy New Year, Judith," he said, smiling. □

H   113

Like Daughter

Like Mother

I DIDN'T recognise Jonathon Forbes as he stood in the scant shelter of my rain-drenched porch with an armful of school-books under his arm.

"Yes?" I inquired, hoping he was not a double-glazing salesman.

"I'm — er — Philippa's English master," he said, a bit hesitantly. "Perhaps you don't remember me?"

Enlightenment dawned!

"I'm so sorry, Mr Forbes. It's the bad light. Of course I recognise you. Please come inside. You're getting frightfully wet."

He came inside, shaking himself free of clinging raindrops. I remember how kind and helpful he'd been on the Open Day I'd attended at my daughter's school a few weeks ago.

He grinned, a bit apologetically. "I called to see how Philippa is progressing, and to bring along a few school books. It would be a pity if she fell behind now with the exam so near."

"How kind of you! She's improving but she has to keep her leg up for quite a while yet."

There was a short pause, then he said, "Do you think I could see her for a few moments?"

"Of course. She's upstairs resting, not in bed, just lying on the bed. Being more or less immobile is not awfully easy for Philippa. I expect you know how much sport means to her."

"I do indeed," he said, following me up the stairs.

"Here's Mr Forbes come to see you," I announced to my scarlet-faced child, who had hastily dragged the duvet over her plastered leg and was obviously overwhelmed with embarrassment by the turn of events. Her expression as she met my eyes was full of agonised appeal.

"Hello, Philippa!" The hesitancy had vanished, and the competent schoolmaster had taken over. "I'm sorry to hear about your accident. What rotten luck."

by GAYE WILSON

He dumped the pile of books on the bedside table. "I've brought you a bit of homework, mainly reading, but it should make catching up easier."

"Thanks, Mr Forbes."

"You should have plenty of time," he resumed briskly, lifting one of the volumes. "Suppose we give Hardy's 'Tess' a trial? And I'd like you to write a short essay on the theme."

The colour in my daughter's face was slowly receding, but there was something in her eyes which made me anxious. They were liquid with emotion, and my heart sank. She wasn't the first teenager to fall in love with her teacher.

I remembered she'd mentioned that he was the idol of every girl in her class, and the significance of this had evaded me until this moment.

My voice was a shade cool as I showed him out of the door.

"Thank you for coming," I said, a bit stiffly. "I'm sure Philippa will benefit from a bit of homework. It was kind of you to think of her."

"Your daughter is one of our most promising pupils, Mrs Carmichael," he replied with equal stiffness. "It's a great disappointment to a teacher to have a failure in his lists. I'm sure you understand the situation."

He gave me a small, formal bow, reached for his raincoat, and vanished into the streaming night.

WHEN he'd gone, I made coffee for Philippa and myself and took it upstairs.

She was sitting upright on the bed glaring at herself in the hand mirror.

"Mummy, how *could* you?" she wailed.

"How could I what?"

"Bring *him* into my bedroom!"

"Well, you weren't alone. I was close behind."

She gave a snort of disgust. "You don't even begin to understand!"

"No, I'm afraid I don't," I said. "What have I done that's so dreadful?"

"Don't you see? Just look at me! I look awful — a mess. Look at my hair, and these spots on my chin. Whatever would he think?

"Why didn't you ask him to call back later, so that I could have had time to — " She broke off.

"Time for what?"

"To make myself look decent . . ."

I sighed and put the coffee tray down. "You don't look a mess, Philippa. You look very nice and very pretty. Nobody would notice those few spots on your chin. It's your age. I don't suppose Mr Forbes would be interested in your chin, anyway."

She turned the mirror this way and that, and lay back on her pillows with a long-drawn-out sigh. "Pass me my coffee, will you or maybe — "

She hesitated. "Perhaps I shouldn't drink coffee any more."

"Why not, for goodness' sake?"

"It's not awfully good for the complexion. Mineral water with a slice of lemon might be better."

"Well, risk it this time as I've bothered to make it," I commented dryly.

Then she was a little girl again! "But Mummy, don't you think he's marvellous? You wait until I tell Jane Price he's been to see me here at home.

"She'll be absolutely green with envy. The whole class will be. Do you think he'll come again?"

"Listen, Phili," I said gently. "Mr Forbes is your teacher. He came tonight out of the goodness of his heart because he doesn't want you to fail your coming exam. If you do, it could reflect on his teaching.

"He's not interested in you personally. He's interested in the success of his pupils as a whole."

A sullen expression settled on the fresh, young face in front of me.

"Oh you," she grumbled, putting her half-finished coffee on the bedside table and glowering at it.

Then she turned peevish. "You don't know how much my ankle hurts tonight. You've no idea the pain I'm suffering."

She was overwrought and I could see near to tears.

"I'm so sorry, darling. Look, I'll get you a bowl of warm water for your hands and face, and you can use some of that rose-perfumed soap Granny brought you. Then I'll make you comfy for the night."

As I tucked her up later, I said deliberately, "I expect Mr Forbes will call again. After all, he'll want to see what you've done.

"He told me you're one of his most promising pupils. You don't want to let him down, do you?"

The glow in her eyes was my reward. "Did he really say that? You're quite sure? You're not having me on?"

"I'm not having you on," I said as I kissed her, and I thought, puppy love is something we all have to suffer.

I didn't suppose it would hurt Philippa any more than it would hurt any other teenager. It was just that she was specially vulnerable at the moment.

I'd tried so hard to protect her from Clive's desertion, but she'd been shocked and distressed almost beyond belief and for a time her whole personality had changed. The past two years had been stressful for both of us, and Philippa was only just beginning to revert to normal.

JON FORBES didn't call again for a couple of weeks, and in the meantime Philippa wrote and re-wrote her essay on the Thomas Hardy book which she was beginning to understand and appreciate.

"Poor Tess." She sighed one evening as we sat together discussing the re-issue of the film on television. "To be not only unloved and rejected, but to be homeless, too."

She shuddered. "We're lucky even without Daddy because we have each other and a nice home."

She was silent for a while, then she got up and gave me a hug.

"When I'm grown-up, I'll look after you, Mummy." She waved her much-thumbed essay. "I'll work so hard you won't have to wait very long, either."

"There's nothing I really want," I assured her, "except to see you happy and settled and independent. Independence is a most necessary thing, Philippa. Don't despise it."

Suddenly she changed the subject.

"Do you think I dare ask Mr Forbes to sign my plaster?" She giggled.

I couldn't help smiling. One moment she was a little girl, and the next — a woman.

When the English master did re-appear, Philippa was hobbling around on crutches. Fortunately we'd just managed a shampoo for her, and she looked quite lovely with little, russet tendrils clustering on her forehead.

I saw him glance at her thoughtfully, then everything was business-like as they discussed the work he wished her to undertake and what she had already done.

"I'm hoping to get back to school pretty soon," she was telling him as I arrived with a tray of coffee and biscuits, and he seemed as pleased as we were at the news.

I breathed a sigh of relief, for I was sure that once my daughter was back with her friends, her passion for the English master would burn itself out in the manner of most schoolgirl crushes.

But there was bad news. The ankle, which had appeared to be progressing satisfactorily, was not. There was a setback which involved additional complications and made it necessary for a further period of leg-rest.

During this difficult time, I was more than grateful to Jon Forbes, for he appeared from time to time always with something to distract and occupy a very bored teenager.

Slowly my fears abated, and I felt I could leave them together in order to catch up with my own work — typing out a manuscript for a Professor of Anatomy who was writing a very dull book. I did not enjoy the job at all, but stuck it out because it was something I could do at home.

When Philippa went off to university, I promised myself I would resume my interrupted career in the commercial art world.

Then one evening Jon Forbes did something quite unexpected. I was in the kitchen washing up a great pile of dishes, when he came in, picked up a tea-towel and started to dry.

"It's all right," I said. "I can manage."

"Sit down, Barbara," he said quietly, "and put your feet up. You look worn out."

I was surprised at his use of my christian name and found myself protesting further. "It's really all right. I'm used to managing."

"I know," he said, "too used to managing."

After that he often left Philippa when he'd set her a problem to work out, and I began to look forward to these pleasant little interludes in my rather uneventful day. We found ourselves discussing many things as well as the academic prowess of my teenage daughter.

He spoke of the death of his wife in a road accident, and I told him of Clive's desertion.

"Philippa took it very badly," I said. "For a while I think she blamed me — maybe rightly.

"Clive was such fun, and they shared a great love of sport. He took her to all the local sporting events, and taught her all she knows."

"Is he in touch?"

"He writes, but he's in Australia now. He would like Philippa to visit them out there, but so far I've hesitated to allow her to go."

"Why?" he asked gently. "Are you afraid she won't come back?"

"I suppose I am, in a way," I admitted. "He has so much to offer her, and I have so little."

He was silent for a while, then he let his arm rest across my shoulder, giving me a little squeeze of sympathy. Neither of us saw the shadow in the doorway nor heard the small scraping movement which must have taken place, but it soon became apparent after he had gone that something had upset Philippa.

"Don't you like kedgeree any more?" I asked as she pushed her supper away fretfully. The answer was a flood of tears and a rush of absurd accusations.

"I saw you!" she stormed. "You and Jonathon."

"Whatever do you mean?" I cried, for I had forgotten the brief incident of the half-caress.

"In the kitchen when he was pretending to help you wash up the dishes! I hopped across on one leg because he was away for such a long time."

CHRISTMAS COMING . . .

I'm becoming very worried now,
As Christmas-time draws near,
We've just moved into this house,
Will Santa know we're here?

I'm sure the roof is much too steep
For reindeer to land upon,
I'm worried they might hurt themselves,
As they slide off, one by one.

And we don't have a chimney now,
So how will Father Christmas
Bring his sack into the house?
Do you think he'll have to miss us?

On Christmas Eve I'll stay awake,
And watch for Santa Claus!
I'll guide him down on to the lawn,
And then take him indoors.

He can sit beside the fire,
Drink tea and eat mince pie.
I'm sure he'll fill our stockings up,
Before he says "Good-bye!"

— Jo Coatswith.

"He *was* helping me wash the dishes," I protested.

"With his arm around your shoulders?"

"Oh Phili, grow up! You've got it all wrong. I'd just told him about Daddy, and his gesture was purely one of sympathy — of understanding. How could you have thought it was anything else?"

I must have convinced her for she sat up, blew her nose and said, "Cross your heart?"

"If you like," I said shortly, "although of course it isn't necessary. As you've told me yourself, Mr Forbes is a very kind, understanding man.

"He has empathy — if you know what that means — and he was just sorry at the way things have been going. You mustn't be so quick to jump to conclusions. It could cause misunderstandings and unhappiness."

The little girl was back again now. "Oh Mummy, I'm sorry. For a moment, I thought you had betrayed me."

I couldn't help a wry smile at her choice of verb, but I kissed her, handed back the cooling plate of kedgeree and began to tidy the room for the night.

Philippa's attitude put a blight on my new-found friendship. She was depressed, her ankle had failed to heal and her attachment to Jon Forbes seemed to be the only bright spot in her life.

I shrank from telling him what had happened — that my daughter was suffering from a fit of jealousy because of his small gesture towards me. What better way of sending him out of both our lives for ever?

I had to think of something else, to discourage any sort of friendship between us. It was a heartbreaking charade to enact, because I realised those small, kitchen interludes had become precious to me in a way I couldn't explain.

I started off by making sure the dishes were washed and stacked away by the time he arrived, and I made a point of never being out of the room with the two of them alone for more than a few minutes.

It didn't take long for the penny to drop. Several times, I caught him looking at me in a puzzled sort of way, especially when I forced myself to talk light-hearted nonsense which only Philippa thought funny.

His eyes were full of questions which I didn't give him a chance to put into words, and as though through mutual consent our small tête-à-têtes ceased altogether.

No longer was the atmosphere free and friendly as we drank our coffee together, for I sensed my daughter was watchful and our visitor uneasy. Yet he kept coming, and although our relationship had changed, I knew that the two of us were intensely aware of each other.

I knew, too, that in different circumstances, he was a man I could have loved, and sometimes I was sure the feeling was reciprocated.

THEN the doctor insisted Philippa should go back into hospital for an intensive course of advanced physiotherapy.

At this she became more depressed than ever, convinced that her sporting days were over.

"Suppose I'll never be able to dance again?" she wailed. "Or skate, or ski or — or anything?"

She'd had a very rough time, and my heart went out to her. I knew I was inclined to spoil her, although I tried not to, and I was amazed that the English master still continued to visit us.

Together we took her into hospital, and on the way home he stopped the car at a pretty country inn where he said they served a particularly delicious supper.

"Thanks for everything," I said a bit shakily when we arrived back home.

I was determined not to invite him in for coffee, for I wasn't sure how strong I could be with the two of us entirely alone for the first time ever.

By this time, I had admitted — but only to myself — that I loved him deeply, ardently and, I was sure, lastingly.

"How long are you going to keep me waiting, Barbara?" he asked gently, as we sat in the car outside my front door. "Are you going to allow a somewhat spoilt little girl to rule your life? Rule both our lives?

"In quite a short time she won't need you as much. She'll have her own life to live. You might even become an encumbrance."

"I thought you were fond of her," I said defensively. "You came to see her in the first place."

"No, my darling. I came to see you."

"But you didn't even know me!"

"Oh yes, I did. I fell in love with you the first time I saw you, at the school Open Day. Remember?

"Philippa's accident was an opportunity to get to know you better. Surely you can't think I'd have designs on a girl young enough to be my daughter?"

He put his arms round me then and rested his cheek against mine. It made me feel warm and happy and secure.

He lifted my hand and placed a kiss inside the palm.

When he spoke, his voice was full of tenderness. "Love like ours has a keeping quality."

Then he helped me out of the car, escorted me to my front door and drove away with a cheerful wave.

★ ★ ★ ★

The next time we visited Philippa we were informed she would be discharged the following weekend.

"We'll have to tell her now," I said as we drove home.

"Tell her what?"

"About us."

"I can't see that as a problem."

"She — she won't like it, Jon. She'll be upset."

"She'll understand, Barbara. She's not a child."

It was clear he had no idea of Philippa's devotion to himself. "We'll tell her we hope to marry as soon as it can be arranged," he decided.

"Oh Jon!" I said. "Just like that?"

"How else?"

"You don't understand. She'll be terribly upset . . ."

He pulled my head on to his shoulder and stroked my hair. "I'm sorry, darling. What a selfish brute I am. Of course I understand. The point is, what can I do about it?

"Suppose," he said slowly, "I arrange to be away for a week or so? It would give you time to prepare her a bit. Would that help?"

"Bless you, Jon, I think it might." Suddenly I wanted to cry.

He insisted on accompanying me to the hospital to fetch Philippa home. She was in great spirits and flung her arms about us both in turn.

"I couldn't believe it when Barry Bradfield gave me the good news!" she cried.

"Who's he?" Jon queried with a grin.

"My physio. He's super, absolutely brill. I told you about him. He'll be doing my out-patient treatment, too. He says I'll be as good as new!"

We stopped at the same little country inn on the way home.

Philippa ate an enormous meal, and chatted gaily until we got home. Then she fell strangely silent and said she'd like an early night.

"It's been a big day for you," I said as I tucked her up.

"So," Jon said, as we stood on the doorstep preparatory to his departure, "I'll stay away until I get the all clear. Don't keep me waiting too long."

"I won't."

JON'S unselfish, understanding action gave me time to think, to sort out my mixed emotions and to plan.

Philippa accepted his absence without comment. I wondered if perhaps she was more mature than I'd given her credit for.

We went for little walks together and attended her hospital sessions.

She would come out from these glowing with optimism. "You know, Mum, there was a time when I thought I'd be permanently crippled. It made Barry laugh — he couldn't understand me even thinking of such a possibility. Sometimes I wanted to die."

"Oh darling," I said, hugging her. "I wish you'd told me."

There were other signs of growing maturity about Philippa, too. She stopped calling me "Mummy," and her choice of reading changed. Perhaps telling her about Jon and me wouldn't upset her after all.

I decided to risk it, and sent Jon the agreed "signal."

"Would you like me to tell Philippa?" he asked gently.

I nodded.

"Then you pop across to the off-licence and get a bottle of champagne. When you return, we'll be ready to celebrate!"

When I got back to the house, champagne glasses were set out on the table. Both Jon and Philippa were grinning.

"Congratulations!" she cried, hugging me, as Jon popped the cork.

It was an unbelievably wonderful evening. All my worries seemed to have evaporated at once. In the middle of it, there was a telephone call for Philippa which lasted a very long time and sent her back to the celebration with heightened colour and very bright eyes. Somehow I refrained from questioning her.

"Wonder what that phone call was all about?" I said to Jon later when we were alone.

"I can tell you," he answered, "because I'm in the know. The inevitable has happened — your daughter has fallen in love!"

"How? Where?" I stammered. "She's not been mixing with any boys for weeks."

"He's not exactly a boy, but he's young enough. His name is Barry Bradfield and apparently he's absolutely wonderful at his job. And in many other ways, too!" □

Glorious Gardens
Priorwood, Melrose

PRIORWOOD lies in the shadow of Melrose Abbey, whose picturesque ruins date from the time of King David I. Indeed, as its name suggests, it was once part of the Abbey gardens, and it is a fitting touch that Priorwood's pleasant orchard should contain species dating back to mediaeval times.

Priorwood's uniqueness today, however, is as a centre for dried flowers. Suitable blooms are picked from the borders and then dried, pressed or preserved in glycerine before being sold in the garden shop.

AS she rose from her desk, Jill knew without looking round that a dozen pairs of eyes were watching her movements.

Over the past two weeks it had developed into a kind of daily ritual, and it amused her so much that she deliberately over-played her part. Stopping at one of the windows she made a big thing of gazing fondly into the car park below.

The inevitable quip soon followed.

"Well, is it still there, Jill?" Sandra Craig made her usual teasing comment.

But today, Viv Peters joined in. "Not much danger of anyone stealing that thing!"

The remark had all the biting sarcasm the others had come to expect from someone known throughout the department as "Vinegar Viv." It was followed by a chorus of jeers.

Jill merely smiled.

"It may not be much, but it's mine," she declared contentedly. "Bought and paid for."

"If you ask me, that car salesman saw you coming." Viv seemed determined to have the last barbed word.

"No-one asked you!" Sandra rose to Jill's defence, and gave her friend a consoling wink.

Jill remained totally unperturbed. She had no illusions about her six-year-old car, and she was the first to admit that it was anything but perfect.

But what else could a girl on her salary afford? Besides, a girl has a right to feel proud of her first car, whatever it looked like.

Viv Peters had not given up. "Are you still going to Bolton on Saturday in that thing?"

The question was loaded with scepticism.

"Of course."

Viv jeered, "If you're not in on Monday, we'll know you didn't make it."

Again there was a howl of protests from the other girls.

"Don't listen to her, Jill," Bette Lamont cried.

"Sour grapes," Sandra declared. "You show her, Jill."

JILL made a show of her indifference as she returned to her desk, but Viv's last remark had struck a sensitive nerve.

Saturday would be the first real test for her car. A hundred-mile round trip was a lot different from the 20-minute drive to and from work.

CHALLENGE ON FOUR

She stubbornly fought off the doubt. Bolton was hardly the far north. Why shouldn't she do it?

When she had driven her dad there and back, he, too, would be finally convinced that she had not been reckless with her savings.

Of course, it was natural he should be concerned. He wasn't the first father to worry about his only daughter driving around in what some had already called an "old banger."

But if her mum could accept and share in Jill's obvious pride and pleasure, why couldn't he?

This made the drive to Bolton so important. It would be the final proof that her car was sound and reasonably reliable.

As she left the office that

**by
CATHIE
MITCHELL**

WHEELS

night, Jill encountered a problem she now had to share with other motorists. It was in the formidable shape of a pick-up truck parked squarely in front of her car, blocking any movement.

For a long moment she stared in disbelief. How could anyone be so idiotic to leave a vehicle like that?

She stretched on to her toes and peered into the driver's cab. The window was down. The seat, well-worn she noted, was empty.

Her brown eyes frantically searched the rapidly emptying car park, but there was no-one who looked as if he might be the driver of this ugly monstrosity.

Within minutes the car park had almost emptied. The sight of her car trapped in all that wide space by the truck heightened Jill's impatience. In a flash of irritation she reached into the cab and stabbed at the horn.

The sound made her jump. Alarmed, she looked round anxiously, fully anticipating a stampeding crowd come to investigate the awful noise.

No-one came. Lights were going out in the office windows. A stillness was settling over the area as buildings emptied of their staff.

Thankfully, Viv Peters would have left by the front of the building. Jill could well imagine what she would have made of this!

At last he came, a huge fellow in a badly-stained boiler suit topped by an almost equally oil-marked face, out of which shone the brightest blue eyes Jill had ever seen.

She couldn't tell if he looked contrite, irritated or just plain obstinate, not with all those smudges on his face, then he grinned.

"Sorry. Had to rush to catch the people in that office before they close. Haven't kept you long, have I?"

Jill looked at her watch deliberately. "Just about twenty minutes!"

"Surely not?"

Jill felt like stamping a foot in annoyance, preferably burying the heel into his big toe! But by the look of his boots it would be her heel that would suffer most. "I'm not in the habit of telling lies! Next time I hope you'll show a bit more consideration for other motorists."

The blue eyes swept over her car, then came back to her. She had the most awful feeling that he was laughing at her and her car.

His next words confirmed this. "Thought that old thing had been abandoned."

He must have spotted the tightening around her mouth and the flash in her eyes.

The smile faded quickly. "Sorry. Just a little joke."

That's just what it was. A little joke! Jill hit back as hard as she could. There was a limit to the number of remarks she was prepared to accept about her car.

"Ouch!" The young man grunted and hurried into the truck.

The still air was shattered by its thunderous roar as he swung it in a wide arc around the car park, gave a parting blast on his horn and was gone.

Challenge On Four Wheels

Jill knew her dad would have been fretting, and this brought an irritating reminder of the cause.

"Problems with the car?"

"Not my car, Dad," she hastened to reassure him. He had still to be convinced that she had done the right thing. "Some idiot had parked right across me. I couldn't move."

He shook his grey head. "No pleasure in driving today."

Jill bit her lower lip. Dad didn't need much prompting to start on one of his pet theories.

"Roads are far too congested. Can't think why you were so keen to get into that lot. Nothing but problems with a car."

"Don't you listen to him, dear," Jill's Mum cut in briskly as she emerged from the kitchen with three steaming plates on a tray.

"Have you forgotten what it's like to be young? How often did you say you wished you could afford a car?" she reminded her husband.

"Different when we were young," he muttered. "Plenty of room on the roads then."

Mum brushed his argument aside with a laugh. "Just get off your hobby-horse and come sit at the table. You too, Jill."

At five o'clock the following day, Jill found herself scanning the car park. No pick-up truck! Was she relieved? Or was there a slight tinge of disappointment tugging at her?

She tossed her long, fair hair dismissively. As if she would wish for a repeat of what happened last night, she told herself.

And yet, there had been something engaging about those bright, blue eyes and the mischievous grin. Pity she couldn't tell what the face looked like under all that oil and grease.

A T last it was Saturday, the day when Jill hoped to allay finally her dad's lingering doubts about the car. She had persuaded him to let her drive him to Bolton for a bowls match.

When he had done the journey in less than half the time it would have taken by public transport, surely then he would concede the wisdom of her purchase?

It was a glorious day. Jill rose early, washed and polished the car.

They were to leave at noon, and Mum was going with them. She and Jill would spend the afternoon shopping in Bolton while Dad played his important game.

At last, Jill got in, switched on the ignition and was rewarded with a weak cough from under the bonnet.

Dad was coming out of the house, ready for the off. He stopped half way down the path.

Jill threw him a quick and hopefully reassuring smile then tried again. The cough sounded even weaker.

Mum's face appeared at the window, looking slightly anxious.

Dad glanced back at her, shrugged his shoulders and approached the car. "What's wrong, love?"

"I — I'm not sure."

Panic was rising like a flood inside her. This was to be her big moment. She could almost feel tears starting to sting her eyes, as she repeatedly twisted the ignition key and each time got less and less response.

She felt her dad's hand on her shoulder as he reached through the open window. His brown eyes weren't accusing, but soft and understanding.

"Sounds like the battery, love. Nothing too serious."

"It still won't start, will it?" Jill threw the words back at him, anger and frustration making her voice sound sharper than she had intended. "And you have to get to Bolton by two."

"Still plenty of time." He straightened. "Just you sit tight for a bit."

"Where are you going?"

"Young lad by the name of Jeff Harper has set himself up in that old workshop round in Tain Street. Heard he's a good mechanic. I'll fetch him."

"But it's Saturday, Dad. He won't be there now."

"He will. Keen as mustard to get himself started. You just hold tight."

KIND THINGS

You tell me so often
You love me —
Without any word being said.
Like leaving the car
For my shopping,
Or bringing up tea in bed.
You say "flowery phrases"
Are simply NOT YOU,
So I'll love you
My love
For the kind things
You do.
                    — Poppy Field.

Challenge On Four Wheels

Jill watched her dad go off briskly down the street, gave up on the car and went back into the house.

Mum had the kettle almost boiling. "We may as well have a cup of tea while we're waiting, dear."

Despite the frustration of it all, Jill found herself smiling faintly at how calmly her mum and dad were accepting the situation.

Then Jill heard the unmistakable roar of a heavy engine. She ran to the window and almost froze in horror. It was the very same truck!

There he was, jumping down from the cab. Very large and unmistakable, even if he was now in jeans and T-shirt.

The vehicle had stopped alongside her car, and any last doubts vanished when she saw her dad also emerge from the cab.

She watched them bend over her car, and had a sudden, almost uncontrollable urge to dash upstairs to her bedroom. Why did it have to be him, of all people!

She could not see his face yet, but she could well imagine that mocking grin. No doubt he was even now making some caustic remark to her dad, undermining his already shaky confidence.

That did it! Jill drew herself erect, set her chin squarely, and marched briskly down the path to the front gate.

"Here's Jill now," her father said.

Jeff Jarper straightened as he turned to meet her.

How strange that his face should be almost exactly as Jill had imagined it — not particularly handsome, more rugged and strong. The eyes were still that marvellous blue and they watched her approach with the laughter she had fully expected.

"Hello there! Thought I recognised the car."

"I thought you had another name for it!" Judy could not disguise the edge in her voice.

His eyebrows rose to disappear under the lock of tousled, blond hair across his forehead. The smile faltered somewhat.

"I said I was sorry about that, didn't I?"

Her dad was looking at them curiously. "You two know each other?"

"We have met," Jill said briefly.

The grin was widening again. "Our paths have crossed." Jeff Harper chuckled.

Then, abruptly, he was serious. "What seems to be the trouble?"

"It just won't start," her dad told him.

The blue eyes focussed on Jill. "Release the bonnet, will you?"

Jill got into the car and did as requested. When Jeff Harper disappeared behind the raised bonnet, she stole a quick look in the mirror. Her cheeks were bright red.

"Idiot!" she told her reflection. "Don't let this big oaf upset you!"

"Try starting it." His shout came to her.

She responded by turning the key and got a low stutter from the engine.

"Battery's flat." Jeff Harper came round from behind the bonnet.

I

"Stay where you are. I'll give you a jump-start."

She watched him rummage in the back of his truck, then pull out two cables which he quickly connected between the vehicles.

"I'll give you a shout when to try it again," he told her.

A moment later the powerful roar of the truck engine filled the quiet street.

"OK. Now try it." His yell came to her above the noise.

Jill turned the key, and all her pent-up emotions were released as her car revved into life.

Jeff Harper removed the cables, slammed shut the bonnet of the car and grinned at Jill.

"Keep her running and you'll be fine." He paused. "Your dad tells me you're driving to Bolton this afternoon. That right?"

"Any reason why we shouldn't?" Jill threw the question back at him almost defiantly.

"Best thing you could do." He nodded. "A run like that should give the battery a good charge."

Jill felt ashamed of her initial anger. "Thanks. What do I owe you?"

"For that? Nothing." He hesitated. "Tell you what you can do."

SOMETHING in his tone set her on guard again. "If you say I should get rid of it — "

Again his eyebrows disappeared under the mat of thick hair. "Certainly not. Got a nice little car there. Just needs a bit of work."

He grinned. "My rates are very reasonable."

Jill had to smile.

"I'll take you up on that," she promised.

"Good. We can talk about it tonight."

"Tonight!"

"When you get back, run your car round to my workshop. It's in Tain Street. I want to charge the battery overnight."

He was walking away again when he stopped to look back at Judy. "Do you like Chinese food?"

"Chinese! Y-yes — "

"Me too. See you later then."

He gave her a final wave, then drove off in his now familiar roar of thunder.

"Good lad that," her dad grunted. "Straight to the point and no nonsense."

"I noticed," Jill murmured.

"Chap like that is worth getting to know, my girl."

Jill smiled at him. "I believe you're right, Dad."

"What did he say to you anyway? About the car, I mean?"

"Wants me to run it round to his workshop when I get back."

Her dad looked relieved. "Good. It shows he's pretty sure we will get back."

Jill burst out laughing. "I certainly hope so, Dad. I love Chinese food." □

by VERONICA
RAFFERTY

A WILD and beauti-
ful place it was —
but lonely! It seemed
like the end of the world
in winter, when the bitter
wind blew up from the
Atlantic and not a single tree
there to shelter the old lighthouse
and the cottage cowering beside it
on the headland.

But in summer — ah, it was different then, with the sun warming
the freshly-painted walls — so bright and white it dazzled the eyes. A
long, steep slope of springing green turf stretched down towards flat,
terraced rocks, where a few tourists with a taste of adventure used to
stretch out, sunbathing and watching the sea attacking the next level
of rocks below.

Even on fine days, the waves crashed fiercely around the rocky
peninsula which seemed to jut out bravely and defiantly — delighting
in its fortress-like position.

Mollie McCann had come to this place as a bride and had lived
there for 40 years, through periods of happiness, contentment,
depression, loneliness and, finally, a great weariness.

Her husband, Seamus, was happy all the time, for he was that kind

Too Soon The Dream

of man. It was a good marriage and they had four fine children — all
of them married now and living in different parts of Ireland. So now
they were together, as they had been in the beginning, but it wasn't
quite the same, of course.

Seamus had warned her, before they married, that it was a hard,
lonely life he was offering her, and she had said that she understood
— but she didn't. She only knew that if he had asked her to go with
him to the ends of the earth, she would have gone gladly and never
stopped to count the cost.

Now she was 60, and he a couple of years older — but not ready
for the gold watch yet, he said. The lighthouse had been his life for
40 years and he loved it with all his heart. He said he would like to
be buried right there, under the green turf, with the wild flowers
growing above him. She shivered and told him not to be so morbid,
but it wasn't morbid to him — he had no fear of dying, as she had.

He knew that she wanted to accept the early retirement that he
had been offered, and he knew about her dream of moving back to
Ennis, 30 miles away, where they had both grown up.

She wanted to live in a nice, little house, in a street sheltered from
the wind, with a few trees around. She wanted relatives and old
friends nearby so that she could pop in for a cup of tea.

He viewed the prospect with great sadness, as if it would be like
the end of his life, in a way.

IT was with surprise that Mollie heard Seamus say, one evening, in
September, that he was thinking of "packing it in." He had just
come in for their evening meal and he looked tired and dispirited.

"I'm getting old, Mollie," he said, as he threw his cap on the peg
by the door and tugged his boots off. "I think I'll have to be making
a move."

He looked desolate as he said it.

His wife busied herself ladling out of the soup and cutting chunks
off the newly-baked bread. Her mind was confused between her own
delight at his change of heart and uneasiness at the pain he would
suffer when the day came.

"Well, that's a bit of a surprise — what's brought this on?" she
said, trying to sound casual.

He had started his soup, and seemed disinclined to discuss the
matter further, saying that the weather forecast was bad tonight.

She knew him well enough not to ask further questions. He would
talk about it again — when he was ready.

Sure enough, a good hour later, as a frenzied wind drove the rain
against the windows in noisy gusts, he came back to the subject.
"Mollie, do you remember that day in July, when the English lady
fell on the rocks and broke her leg and we had to haul the stretcher
to the top?"

"I do, indeed — I was more worried about you than the patient,
God forgive me," Mollie said.

"Well, that was the day I began to feel that I wasn't up to the job any more. I always said I wouldn't stay on here past that point.

"After it was over and the poor soul was on her way to Ennis in the ambulance, I got to thinking. If that ambulance driver hadn't been a strapping young fellow, able to do more than his share, we would never have got her to the top," he admitted.

"But Seamus — things like that don't happen every day of the week," Mollie pointed out. "You can't be worrying all the time about things that *might* happen."

"Ah, that's not good enough, girl. In this job you must be able to cope with emergencies — and I'm not sure that I can any more."

FOR a moment, Mollie was at a loss for words. He heart ached for him, who had always been so strong and sure and confident.

No matter how dangerous or difficult the job had been, he had tackled it and he had always succeeded in what he set out to do, through patience and stubborn determination. He had combined the duties of lighthousekeeper with those of a lifeguard, a medical orderly, a mechanic, an electrician, a guardian angel to children — and a host of other things as well.

Mollie couldn't think of the right words with which to comfort him, although they were so close in understanding. Instead, she put an arm around his shoulders and hugged him.

"You're tired, love," she said. "Off to your bed now — get a good night's sleep and you'll feel better in the morning."

Mollie felt strangely insecure as she cleared away the remains of the meal. Never, in all their married life, had she felt anything really depended upon her. It was always a case of, "Seamus will see to that — put this right — decide what's best to do . . ."

She realised how much she had come to depend upon him — far too much. She thought of all the trivial, domestic problems that she had faced him with, through the years.

Why hadn't she dealt with them herself? She was perfectly capable. She had accepted all that he had to offer and taken it as her right.

Oh, she had loved him well enough, but was that enough? Had she supported him, helped him with *his* problems and understood the pressures of his job sufficiently?

She was honest enough with herself to admit that she had not. She had taken him for granted, but perhaps it wasn't too late to reverse rôles.

She finished the washing-up, and as she came back to the dying fire, she stopped at the sideboard and looked at their wedding photo on the wall above. She saw a slim, pretty girl, her face alight with love.

Her bridegroom — a good nine inches taller, looked down at her devotedly, protectively. Their arms were entwined and their hands tightly clasped.

Mollie was aware, as never before, that the love she had felt for Seamus, in that moment, was only a shadow of what she felt now. She sat in his old rocking-chair until there was no spark left in the fire, and the kitchen grew cold. Then she got up and moved noiselessly into the bedroom.

MOLLIE woke around three o'clock. Her brain seemed to leap into action before her eyes were open. She got up without disturbing Seamus — he lay in a deep, exhausted sleep — and went into the kitchen to make some tea.

Then, putting the light out, she sat at the window and pulled back the curtains. She picked up the wool shawl one of the girls had sent her for her birthday and wrapped herself in it.

Then she sipped her tea and looked out, trying to see the scene with her husband's eyes.

This was the place Seamus loved, and it would break his heart to leave it — too soon. But what about her — did she not deserve consideration, too?

She hadn't felt the loneliness so keenly until the last child had married and gone away, and she didn't have so much to do any more and she had too much time to think — about another kind of life, a life that *she* would choose.

Was it selfish to want to live like other people? Seamus seemed ready now to give in and take his well-earned retirement, so why didn't she feel happy and elated?

Tomorrow she would encourage him to take action. They would probably let him go at Christmas, and they could be settled back in Ennis by the New Year. That had been her dream for so long — so why did it not have the power now to give her contentment and peace?

The answer was as clear as the calm moon, and it lit up her mind as surely as the moonlight carved its path of light across the water. She could only have peace if Seamus was happy. Ennis would be nothing to her if his heart was still here — and it would be.

Mollie closed the curtains and went back to bed with a quiet mind.

★   ★   ★   ★

Seamus awoke at dawn. Mollie was sleeping peacefully. He went into the kitchen quietly, to make some tea and have a think — the two things often went together. He pulled open the curtains and sat beside the window with his mug of tea and two biscuits.

The sky was clear, after the night storm, and the eastern horizon was streaked with gold and pink on a the backcloth of purest, palest turquoise. The skies were a never-ending source of delight to Seamus.

He listened to the waves breaking on the rocks and the cry of the gulls as they swooped down from their night perches on the cliffs, and he knew that leaving here was going to be the hardest thing he had ever done.

But apart from his loss of confidence in his ability to tackle all aspects of the job, he was aware of Mollie's feelings.

The wild beauty of this place which set his soul rejoicing only made her lonely and fearful. The time had come to go — sooner than he had expected — but at least it would make one of them happy.

A FEW hours later, when the peat fire was burning steadily and the bacon and eggs sizzling and the kettle singing, the discussion was re-opened.

Mollie had the first innings and what she said meant that the careful words rehearsed by Seamus at dawn were quite unnecessary.

"I've been thinking," she said, as she scalded the tea in the brown, earthenware pot, "about what Mr O'Brien from HQ said when he paid us a visit early in the year. Didn't he ask if you would be prepared to take on a trainee here, and didn't you turn it down because you couldn't imagine having another fellow around the place, after all this time on your own?"

Seamus agreed, guardedly.

"Well, I think that's why you were offered early retirement, because they *need* people like you to train the young ones."

"But there's the paper work, Mollie, and I'm not sure that I could tackle that," Seamus protested. "I've never been used to it . . ."

"Don't be telling me that, you great idiot! Of course you could do it! You know you've got more experience than anyone on this coast," Mollie reminded him. "You *should* be passing it on to a young fellow — you've got no right to keep it all to yourself.

"Don't you see, this is the answer! You can take things a bit easier and there'll always be someone to help with emergencies."

★   ★   ★   ★

Mollie cleared the plates away and brought out thick slices of fresh bread and re-filled their mugs. The light of hope was in Seamus's eyes, but there was one more hurdle to overcome — perhaps the most difficult to discuss.

"But, Mollie — what about you? I know you don't really want to stay on. I don't want you being all noble and making sacrifices for me. Anyway, I want you to be happy."

She knew that was true, she had always known it.

This was the bit that might prove difficult for her — she was no good at telling lies, no matter how good the cause. She couldn't say that she had changed her mind and decided she loved this place, after all. Her dream of Ennis was only put aside for a while, not abandoned.

She said, in all honesty, "Seamus, your happiness is all mixed up with my own. I would have none at all if I saw you miserable, so I'll gladly stay here until they kick us both out.

"Now, no more talk — just lift up that phone and tell Mr O'Brien you've changed your mind."

Overcome by the unaccustomed effort of making what was, for her, an emotional speech, Mollie retired to the sink to dry her eyes and wash the dishes, leaving Seamus reaching joyfully for the phone. □

A S the plane began to descend over the airport, the realisation of what I had done was overwhelming! I had abandoned my native land, my family, my job — even my widowed Mum — for the sake of a man I had not even known six months ago.

When I was with him my whole being was filled with glorious certainty, but when we were apart dreadful doubts and uncertainties tormented me.

Would I be able to settle with him in the UK? Would it be so very different from Canada, where I had been born and bred and which I loved?

Alan said I would. He was certain I would find everything compatible, after all — as he put it — there would be no language problems, no religious difficulties, nor indeed serious weather difference.

He was, as usual, entirely logical — a typical computer specialist, determined to go to the top.

Yet he had been unable to settle in my country. Four years had been the limit of his endurance, then an offer from his old firm in London had lured him back on more than willing feet.

"But you love working for Burgess!" I'd cried, when he told me the news.

"Agreed," he'd replied calmly. "But now, Framptons are better."

"But you left them . . ."

"That was several years ago. Things have changed now," Alan had pointed out. "There's been a take-over, and they've developed into a very powerful firm.

"It was sheer luck old Oliver Buckingham remembered me when this vacancy occurred. We

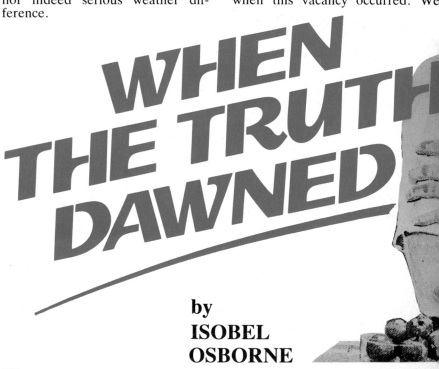

WHEN THE TRUTH DAWNED

by
ISOBEL OSBORNE

always got on well, and he's not far off retirement. He was really upset when I decided to emigrate."

There was quite a long silence between us, and then I'd said, "I haven't met your folks yet. Suppose they don't think I'm a suitable daughter-in-law? Suppose they don't like me?"

"They will," Alan had promised and he'd given me a hug. "They know all about you and are longing to meet you."

"Even so, I would rather we didn't get married until I'm absolutely sure I'll be able to settle."

"OK," he'd agreed with his devastating, crooked smile. "I'll accept that. We'll fly back here for the wedding whenever you're ready. Is that a fair offer?"

He'd folded me in his arms again and kissed me this time, and, as always, I was lost.

I really did love him, and I could understand his wanting to return home. The offer from his old firm must have been very tempting. If this hadn't happened, I was sure he would have stayed in Canada and we'd have settled down there.

THE plane was descending rapidly now, and I could see glittering lights beneath us. I tightened my seat belt as instructed, and prepared myself for far more than the physical bump on landing!

I got through Customs with little delay, and as I emerged into the Arrivals' Lounge my heart was beating rapidly. There were rows of people waiting for friends or loved ones, some holding up placards with names printed on them in large letters.

I couldn't see Alan, which was unusual, for he was a head and shoulders above the average male and I had become used simply to looking up and there he would be!

There was one very tall man scanning the arrivals, but he wasn't Alan. He wasn't the least bit like Alan, apart from his height and the width of his shoulders.

His hair was fair, the colour of wheat, and it flopped over his forehead, schoolboy fashion. His face was weather-beaten and thinner than Alan's.

I put him down as a farmer, when to my surprise his eye seemed to be picking me out.

The waiting crowd began to drift away, but the tall man stayed in his place.Then he began to walk towards me, eyebrows raised and a half-smile lightening his face.

"You *have* to be Carol-Ann," he said, stopping in front of me. "I'm Neil, Alan's brother. He couldn't make it tonight, so he asked me to meet you instead."

A chill of disappointment washed over my whole body.I felt like bursting into tears. What a climax to all the emotional stress to which I had been subjected — my fiancé couldn't even meet my plane.

"It wasn't his fault," Neil continued in a concerned voice. "He got sent off by the firm, and the job took longer than estimated."

I felt slightly better at this explanation, but the anticipated thrill of re-union was swept away.

"It's good of you to stand in for him," I murmured.

"Not at all. It's a great pleasure. Now, let's go and find my car. It's a fair drive home, so I took the liberty of booking a meal for us at a little pub I know of, called The Mill Stream. It's not too far from the airport, but it's the sort of place to warm your heart as well as your stomach."

He was right.The Mill Stream was the most English of English pubs, with a rattered bar, polished brass, Toby jugs, old-world harnesses and a meal fit for a king.

We sat at a small, oak table with two red candles flickering between us, and a genuine log fire warming our backs. If only it had been Alan sitting there opposite to me, my home-coming would have been perfect.

Neil was extremely thoughtful. He kept up a flow of cheery chat, and after I'd eaten and consumed two glasses of excellent wine, my spirits began to rise and I enjoyed the remainder of the drive home.

I think the notice, WELCOME CAROL-ANN, surrounded by fairy lights fixed across the front door, did more for my morale than even Neil's hospitality. It looked so warm-hearted, and as we drew up the door was flung wide and smiling faces and outstretched arms spilled out into the night.

"You must be exhausted, Carol-Ann." Alan's mother hugged me warmly, as did his father and, more timidly, his schoolgirl sister, Cathie.

I was ushered into a bright, cheery room, divested of my outdoor clothing and gently pushed into a massive arm-chair and supplied with a steaming cup of coffee.

"We're so sorry about Alan," his mother (whom I was to call Angela) said. "I know the poor darling must be sick to death about it, but you know what he is where the job is concerned. He'll be home by the weekend, when we're going to have a great big party for the two of you."

My room was as warm and comfortable as the welcome they had given me, and I fell asleep almost immediately, waking to a sunny, autumn day long after the rest of the family were about their business.

I pattered to the window and looked out. Here then were the rolling Downs Alan had so often described to me, reaching far into the distance, with the river like a silver snake threading its way between them.

IT was a breathtaking view. I was standing there drinking it in, when the door opened and Angela appeared carrying a laden breafast tray in her hands.

"Good morning!" She beamed. "I hope you feel rested and hungry for I've brought what is known as a full English breakfast. It's possible you won't be used to this, but Jasper will help you out, if necessary. He's always hungry and in danger of getting fat."

Jasper turned out to be a Beagle, who leapt upon my bed and refused to be budged until he'd been given a taste of my over-large breakfast.

"Where's everybody?" I asked.

"Cathie has left for school, and Dougal for the office. Neil decided to take a day off to stand in for Alan. I hope that will be fine for you? I expect he'll want to take you and Jasper for a long, long walk."

"Lovely," I said. "I'll look forward to that."

Neil was a stimulating companion as we swung along in the breezy sunshine, Jasper rushing hither and thither in a non-stop search for rabbits. He talked mainly of his brother, filling me in with things Alan did when they were both schoolboys.

"He was always the clever one," Neil said. "He was an absolute wizard at maths, and science in general. I'm glad he's managing to use his talents so well, although I'm afraid he's become something of a workaholic."

I laughed. "I'll have to take him in hand. All work and no play — you know the rest. What about you?"

"I'm just a horse-doctor," he said modestly. "I work with my hands — at all times of the day and night."

"A vet? Surely that takes brains, too? What about the training?"

He shrugged his massive shoulders and changed the subject.

When we returned home tired, but strangely contented, a pleasant surprise awaited me. Alan had finished the job and was on his way

Glorious Gardens

The Great Garden of Pitmedden, Grampian.

THE harsh north-east seems a surprising setting for a garden in the French grand manner, but such indeed was the masterpiece created here in 1675 by Sir Alexander Seton. Three centuries later, painstaking research has enabled the National Trust for Scotland to restore Pitmedden to its original magnificence.

Forming its centre are the four *parterres,* their compartments of colourful bedding plants glowing like enamelled jewellery. A collection of 27 sundials mark the passing of time over this aristocrat of gardens.

home. Apparently, he'd phoned just after Neil and I had set out.

"He'll be arriving at the local airport," Neil said. "It's quite near. I'll take you, then I'll shove off. Alan parks his car there, so the two of you can drive home together in the moonlight."

"You're going to miss dinner," Angela pointed out. "You'll have to start in half an hour."

She bustled away, re-appearing almost immediately with a tray. Neil and I had a toasted sandwich each and watched the news on TV until it was time to leave.

Suddenly, as we drove down the leafy lanes which led to the motorway, my apprehension returned, yet I'd felt relaxed and happy walking the hills with Neil and Jasper. I assured myself I was suffering from nerves, and the moment I saw Alan everything would be all right.

"It looks as if the plane's down already," Neil remarked, as we parked the car.

He grinned. "I'd better make myself scarce. Two's company and three's a crowd in present circumstances . . ."

"Thanks for everything," I said, and he gave my hand a quick squeeze and was gone.

The small airport wasn't crowded, and Alan and I spotted each other right away. For a moment I stood frozen to the ground — he looked different somehow, not so tall, and he'd grown what I assumed to be a "designer beard" which I didn't like.

"Carol-Ann!" There was nothing lukewarm about his delight at seeing me, and I felt myself enveloped in an almost lethal hug before he could bear to let me go. "What rotten luck, me being sent away just when you were arriving."

"Couldn't you have talked your way out of it?"

He screwed up his mouth and shook his head. "Wouldn't have been a good idea."

"Well, Neil's filled in wonderfully well," I said rather tartly.

"Good old Neil. He's a great guy. D'you feel like a coffee?"

I'd been hoping he would suggest something a bit more exciting than a coffee.

"Aren't you hungry?" I hinted.

"The plane meal was unusually satisfying — I couldn't eat a thing. What about you?"

"A coffee would be fine," I said untruthfully, and we found a table in the crowded cafeteria.

On the way home, Alan talked excitedly about the wonders of his new job, explaining at length technical details which I tried to understand but couldn't.

I was relieved when at last the lights of home appeared.

Angela, without even asking us, produced two large bowls of home-made soup, which we both consumed with enthusiasm.

I was glad when Neil came home and the family closed in with general discussion and homely gossip, for somehow Alan and I seemed less close to each other than when we had first met. He didn't seem interested in what I was saying — he could talk of nothing but computers.

I noticed Neil glance at him with a sort of amused tolerance.

THE next few days produced an anxiety inside me which I couldn't shake off. Everyone was out at work, or school in the case of Cathie. Even Angela had a part-time job which took up the whole of the afternoons.

I took Jasper for long country walks, and tried to analyse my mixed-up feelings. At last I had to confess that Alan had disappointed me. I wasn't sure whether or not I had disappointed him.

Yet it had seemed so different when we had been together in Canada. Now, I seemed to have fallen out of love with him, and I couldn't think why. Was I just fickle?

Then I knew, and my face burned with shame as I realised the truth. I had fallen in love with Alan's brother! No gathering was complete for me unless he was there, and whenever our eyes met something special seemed to pass between us, something entirely magical. I wondered if he felt the same, or was I imagining the feeling was mutual?

I wanted to go home. I wanted to be by myself for a while, or at least with my own folk. I had a lot of thinking to do. There was no point in shilly-shallying — it wasn't fair to Alan.

At last I plucked up the courage to tell him how I felt, and I'll never forget his reaction.

He grasped me by the shoulders and all but shook me. "You shan't make a fool of me, Carol-Ann! I won't allow it!

"If you want to go home, I'll take you and we'll be married as I promised. We'll have a wonderful honeymoon in the Rockies or somewhere. You're just suffering from wedding nerves."

Then I said an awful thing. "I want to marry a man, not a machine."

I stopped, hand before my mouth. "Oh, Alan, I'm sorry. It's — it's just that computers seem to be the most important things in your life."

"Computers are not only our bread and butter, but they are our jam and cream as well," Alan spluttered, going almost purple in the face. "Don't you want the sort of things money can buy? A high standard of living?"

"I don't know!" I cried wildly. "I'm all mixed-up. I don't know what I want, except to go home."

I burst into tears then and left him staring after me as I rushed from the door.

Angela was wonderful — no disapproval, no tightening of the lips, no word of reproach.

"Thank goodness you've found out before the knot was tied," she said practically. "Don't fret, Carol-Ann. Alan will get over it — he has done before, and he'll learn. His pride has been injured more than his heart, and anyway, hearts mend . . ."

I felt better after my talk with Angela, but of course, I still had to get away. To make matters worse, I had to send home for more money. I hadn't anticipated an immediate return home, and cash was low.

Alan wangled himself a course which took him out of the way for 10 days, which was a welcome respite, and Neil asked me if I'd like to help out at his surgery for a few days.

I loved it there, although my heart ached as I watched him dealing with the animals, and loving him more than I'd thought it possible to love a man. He was so kind and painstaking in all that he did — if only I'd met him first and in other circumstances.

WHEN at last I was able to arrange a return flight, Neil offered to drive me to the airport.

Every inch of that drive was full of pain. How could I have imagined he felt more than friendship for me? I must have been crazy.

We stopped at the same little pub for a meal en route, lunch this time, but I could scarcely swallow the dainty meal he ordered.

"We have over an hour to spare, Carol," he said when we had finished, "and there's somewhere I'd like to take you. It's only ten minutes' drive from here."

The "somewhere" proved to be an animal hospital situated on the outskirts of a small country town.

"I've been offered a senior appointment here," he explained, "only recently ratified."

He took both my hands in his, and lifted them up to his face. "It will mean buying a very small house and living a bit frugally for a while, but it's what I've always dreamed of."

"It sounds — wonderful," I stammered.

He went on, still holding my hands, "And you know what I want to do then?"

I swallowed hard and shook my head.

"I want to come over to Canada and ask you a certain question, a question I can hardly put to you now, for obvious reasons. Do you know what your answer will be, my darling?"

We were standing so close to each other, I could feel his warm breath on my face. I couldn't prevaricate or be facetious, so I buried my face in his shirt, and whispered, "Yes."

He stroked a strand of hair away from my cheek. "I've loved you, Caro Mia, from the first moment I saw you looking lost and bewildered at the airport. Sometimes I've dared to hope . . ."

He kissed me then, and it seemed that I'd waited a lifetime for this moment of perfection.

"It will mean leaving your homeland all over again," he said gently. "Will that be too much to ask?"

I lifted my head then, and looked into his eyes.

"Home is where the heart is," I reminded him, " and that will be wherever *you* are." □

by CHRISTINE PETERS

An

Unlikely Cinderella

M ELODY had been warned about the riverside chill. She arrived at the quayside feeling clumpy and dumpy. Thermal underwear, wellies, quilted coat and woolly hat hardly made for a glamorous image.

However, when she looked at the dark greasy water beneath the shroud of drifting white vapour, she was glad that, Guidelike, she had come prepared.

Despite the cold, there was plenty going on. There was a stimulating hustle and bustle in the atmosphere, cheerful exchanges, an air of purpose amongst the people covering steel skeletons of stalls with red, white and blue-striped awnings and wooden display benches.

She caught sight of Sylvia and made her way over to her.

"It's not very warm, is it?" Sylvia said.

"I'm well wrapped up, as you can see, but I'm sure the sun'll get out."

"It's always freezing here, Melody, even in summer."

Melody doubted if she would notice, with all the clothes she had on!

"What would you like me to do?" she asked.

She helped Sylvia unpack the boxes and trays of cakes. How on earth had she managed to make so much, Melody wondered?

Sylvia must have been up half the night — no wonder she looked so tired these days. Melody couldn't help but admire her determination.

K

The fact that she was a single mother with a badly-handicapped daughter wasn't going to deter Sylvia from keeping her promise to send her little girl to Disneyland as soon as she could.

It had to be soon. Later on could very well be too late, and Sylvia knew that.

"I brought one or two odds and ends I thought might be useful," Melody said, handing over a couple of carrier bags.

"Oh, Melody, they're lovely. Thank you so much." Sylvia laid out the lacy, rainbow-coloured tops with delight. Then she came to the Aran jumper and hesitated.

"You can't really want to put this on the stall and sell it?"

Melody's face twisted for a moment.

"No," she agreed, "I couldn't *sell* it — but I might let it go free to a good home!"

IT was impossible to put a price on the Aran jumper. It held so much that was painful to her, her sweet dreams and bitter disillusionment an integral part of it.

It had taken her a very long time to make it. She'd started it as a labour of love when she'd thought she and Dennis were going to live happily ever after, and finished it as a way of punishing herself, just because she'd started it.

There had not been a fairy-tale ending. Dennis already had a wife and family.

She was getting over it now. The pain had gone. But these days, her emotions seemed frozen, and she kept other men at a distance, reluctant to become involved, unwilling to trust again, only occasionally admitting that she was lonely.

Sylvia giggled suddenly. "It's big, isn't it? You might have been knitting it for the whole rugby team, not just one man in it!"

"Dennis was big enough to be a whole rugby team! Caveman build, you know! Yes, it'll certainly be noticed."

Melody looked around.

Opposite, two men were setting up a gardening stall. One of them seemed familiar. Somewhere before she had seen the big man with the round face, curly hair escaping from a woollen hat.

She realised, and nudged Sylvia. "You didn't tell me Benny came here from 'Crossroads!' "

He glanced over.

Oh, dear, had he heard?

Sylvia smiled at the two men.

"Come and meet my friend," she invited.

Melody was hot with embarrassment. Had he heard? But it was true, he did remind her of the famous Benny.

"This is Melody," Sylvia said. "She's going to look after the stall for me today. I'm going home soon to take Debbie to a special lunch at church for handicapped children. This is Bill."

The smaller, older man smiled and shook Melody's hand.

"And I'm Ben," the younger man said.

An Unlikely Cinderella

He was even larger, close to. His huge hand was dry and rough. It swamped Melody's, making hers seem dainty and fragile.

Melody found herself remembering Dennis's touch. When he had held her hand it had been inviting, electric.

This man's clasp was quite different, firm yet gentle, giving an impression of friendly strength and honesty. His eyes were harebell blue, calm, even lazy but kind and full of laughter.

"You're not really called Ben, are you?"

"No," he admitted, "I'm Dave. Dave Wenlock."

"Melody James."

"Melody. A pretty name for a pretty girl."

"Thank you," Melody said, knowing instinctively he wasn't shooting a line.

She guessed he might tease, but it would only be gently, and she was sure he would always be sincere in what he said.

"We'll give you a hand to dismantle the stall the afternoon," Bill assured her.

"And I'll bring you coffee when you start looking cold," Dave promised.

"I'm sure the sun will get out," Melody said again.

"Oh, it will," Dave agreed, "but you'll still feel cold. The wind's always cutting here."

He smiled and ambled away.

PEOPLE trickled to the quayside market, then the pace quickened. Soon there were floods of them milling around the stalls.

Melody had hoped that Sylvia's stall would be sold out in minutes, but business was slow.

Dave came over. She wondered if he'd noticed her concern.

"Don't worry," he told her. "People are funny. They're wary of newcomers, take time deciding, but they'll come round. Keep a couple of those sultana loaves for me, will you?"

He smiled encouragingly.

He came back later with two mugs of coffee, and Melody was glad of it. The sun was high now, but the river did indeed blow cold air to freeze feet and numb hands, and she wrapped her fingers around the mug, drawing out every scrap of warmth she could.

Dave asked if he could have a bag of ginger snaps, and she gave him one. He sampled a biscuit, then deliberately broke the others in half.

"Hey, these are good!" he said. "Like to try one, kids?"

He held out the bag and children eagerly took up the invitation which somehow included their parents. The biscuits started selling fairly briskly.

He winked at Melody and padded back to his own stall, but she'd got the idea. Small free samples certainly helped her sales. She began enjoying herself.

147

Dave re-appeared with more coffee and bread buns overflowing with beef burgers and hot dogs.

"Ready for lunch?" he asked.

"Oh, how lovely. Yes, please." Melody realised how hungry she was feeling.

Glorious Gardens

Sissinghurst Castle Garden, Kent

TUDOR towers, red brick walls and a moat flanked by azaleas form a romantic background to this garden, set high above the Vale of Kent. It certainly charmed novelist Vita Sackville-West, who, with her husband Sir Charles Nicolson, turned its neglected wilderness into one of the great gardens of this century.

Old-fashioned roses, a nuttery, and an aromatic herb garden delight the senses, while in summer the cottage garden is ablaze with colour. A profusion of figs and vines bring a Mediterranean feel to this quiet corner of the Kentish countryside.

"You don't mind if I join you?" he asked.

"Not in the least."

Melody was surprised to find she really meant it. Eagerly, she bit into one of the buns. The burger was spicy and succulent, the roll fresh and sprinkled with sesame seeds.

"This is super," she said enthusiastically, taking another huge bite.

"Of course," he agreed calmly, his blue eyes laughing. "When I give a young lady lunch, she gets the very best. When you're trying to impress, what else could you possibly offer but something from Sophie's Snack Bar?"

"Are you trying to impress? Whatever for?"

"Because you're the prettiest girl I've ever seen." He smiled roguishly, but Melody knew he meant it.

She found herself colouring. Good heavens, she hadn't blushed for years!

During the afternoon Melody was busy. She was surprised that no-one inquired about the "Free to good home" Aran jumper, though she knew it was far larger than usual. She guessed that people thought there was a catch somewhere, and weren't prepared to be caught.

AT one point she noticed a leather-jacketed young lad, fairly tall but very thin, broomstick legs in tight jeans, his feet monstrous in thick-soled boots, long hair in several garish colours that didn't harmonise.

His manner and appearance were aggressive, but his eyes were long-lashed and gentle, and rested wistfully on the Dundee cakes.

Melody pretended not to notice him going through his pockets, extracting coins and counting them.

"Hey, miss," he said. "Can I have half of one of them?"

"Half?" she echoed stupidly.

"Yes. Well, it's me mum's birthday on Tuesday, see, and she loves them. I can't afford a whole one."

He looked up at her with puppy-like eagerness and trust, and Melody couldn't bear to disappoint him.

"How much are you short?" she asked.

"Fifty-five pence."

She picked up a Dundee cake, put it in a bag, gave it to him and took his money.

He drew back suspiciously, and glared angrily at her. "I don't want no hand-outs. I just want a half. I can pay for a half."

She hadn't meant to hurt his pride.

"Who's giving you a hand-out?" she asked. "I can't cut it in half. Bring the rest next week."

"Honest?" The brown eyes were eager again, his thin face split by a huge grin.

"Honestly," she assured him.

"I'll be back next Sunday," he promised as he swaggered away.

The youth who came a few minutes later was very different. His clothes were similar, his hair close-cropped, but he was bigger altogether and much older.

His eyes frightened Melody. There was nothing soft about them this time — they were cold and shrewd, his mouth hard and unrelenting. He seemed interested in the Aran jumper.

"I'll have that," he said.

"No, you won't," Melody retorted immediately.

She didn't want to keep it, but neither did she want it to go to someone like him, who wouldn't appreciate all the hard work that had gone into it.

"Why not? It says, 'Free To Good Home,' doesn't it?"

He shot her a poisonous look, and Melody knew he knew she was scared, but something deep inside wouldn't let her give in to him. "For one thing it's too big for you, for another I'm not sure you would give it a good home, and I'm certainly not letting it go to someone who can't even say 'please'!"

"There's nothing on that card about saying 'please', is there?" His voice was low, but menacing. "Shouldn't say things are free if you don't mean it, should you?"

"And you shouldn't argue with a lady!"

Dave had materialised behind the youth. One huge hand rested on the lad's left arm, the other held him by the back of the neck.

Gently, it seemed, Dave led him towards the quayside railings, and made him look down at the cold, murky water.

"Should you?" he asked.

"No," the lad agreed sullenly.

"Right. Well, off you go, then, and don't come back."

"I won't forget this!" The lad glowered.

Dave was unperturbed. "Neither shall I, laddie, neither shall I. You remember that!" He looked at Melody. "Nasty piece of work, that one. Are you all right?"

"Yes. Thanks, Dave."

"Any time. Give me a shout if he comes back."

Melody couldn't forget the incident. It had taken the gloss off the day.

A BOUT half past two, Bill and Dave began packing up. Dave came over to see Melody again.

"We're going now," he said. "We've arranged for Pete to give you a hand to dismantle your stall, and I'll be back about four o'clock. I'll pick up what's left and take it to Sylvia's, then drop you off home, if that's all right."

"Yes, fine, thank you. Sylvia said she'd make arrangements, but she went off in such a rush I didn't get a chance to ask what they were. I was going to wait and see what happened."

About quarter past three, the shoppers suddenly melted away, at half past the vendors started clearing their stalls and packing their vans and cars, at four o'clock the quayside was almost deserted though there was a mobile café along at the far end. Probably Sophie's Snack Bar, reflected Melody.

She wandered over to the railings and leaned on them, watching the water swirling by, wondering why she'd enjoyed herself so much.

Was it because it was so different to what she was used to? It had certainly been a lot more interesting than typing statements and invoices.

FOR MORE WONDERFUL READING

Hope you've enjoyed the stories you've read here. If so, you'll be sure to enjoy the heartwarming stories and serials which appear every week in that popular magazine — "The People's Friend."

And there's also cookery, knitting, features and even fun for the kids within its pages.

For information about subscription rates, ask your local newsagent, or write to: Subscribers' Dept., People's Friend, 80 Kingsway East, Dundee DD4 8SL.

Was it the fresh air, not knowing who was coming next or what they'd want, or was it the camaraderie of the stallholders who'd been so helpful and friendly to her? She couldn't imagine Dennis putting himself out in the same way as Dave.

She was a little worried about Dave. Obviously he was interested in her, and though she found him very pleasant, she didn't want any emotional involvement. She wasn't prepared to lower her defences yet!

She didn't know what made her swing round, but when she saw the cold-eyed youth and his two companions she was afraid.

"Your big friend's not here now," he sneered, his voice still low and soft, but just as threatening.

"So?"

"So you'd better hand it over."

"Hand what over?"

"Come off it, lady. You know better than to play games! And hand it over quick, or you'll be the one saying 'please' — when you want us to stop knocking you around."

"You must feel very proud of yourselves. Three to one. Must make you feel very brave and strong!"

"Fair play and all that rubbish?" he scoffed again. "You're wasting your time, lady. Hand it over now, while you've got the chance, or take the consequences."

The sensible thing to do was obey, but something about him fired a defiance in Melody she didn't know she possessed, and she told him to get lost.

They closed in on her, and she began kicking, screaming and scratching. Out of the corner of her eye she saw a car approach, and Dave leap out of it. Farther away, a thin lanky form was running towards them.

She was slammed against the railing with such force she slumped to the ground and lay there powerless, like the stupid heroines in films, only now she knew they weren't so stupid. She couldn't get her breath, felt sick, and her head was ringing.

Her eyes wouldn't focus properly, but she saw Dave was on the ground, and that two of the youths were attacking him. They'll kill him, she thought, trying to struggle to her feet. She saw something glinting but what it was didn't register.

"Look out, Mister, he's got a knife!" another voice yelled.

THERE was a flash of denim and black leather, and a matchstick figure with multi-coloured hair flung himself into the battle. His bony fists pounded furiously, and the seven-league boots were busy, too.

When Melody eventually managed to stand upright, Dave was once more on his feet and in the thick of things.

Suddenly it was all over. The three youths turned and ran.

"Are you all right, Melody?"

"Did they hurt you, Miss?"

"I'm OK, just shaken," she assured her two latter-day knights. Her vision righted itself. "What about you?"

The boy's cheek was grazed, and a knee showed through his jeans, but he would probably consider that fashionable anyway!

Dave had changed into a grey suit and white shirt. His jacket had been ripped, and both it and the shirt were covered with dirt. There was a dark, wet stain on his left sleeve, which was spreading.

"Dave, you're hurt," Melody said, worried. "Let me have a look at it."

"It's only a scratch," he assured her.

"Let me see," Melody insisted.

When she saw the sticky, red patch on the shirt-sleeve, the world suddenly started swaying. She was conscious of Dave's arms around her and the next thing she remembered was being helped inside Sophie's Snack Bar.

"Come in, dear. Sit down. I'll get you a nice cup of tea."

Sophie fussed over her, gave her a bucket-sized mug of sweet tea, and turned her attention to Dave.

"Let's see that arm, Dave. Hmm, nasty cut, but it'll be all right. I'll bandage it for you."

"What about anti-tetanus?" Melody asked. "Shouldn't he go to hospital?"

MOTHER'S DAY

A posy half wilting
From hot little hands,
Midst several offerings lies.
Dandelions, daisies, buttercups, too,
All part of a splendid surprise!
And the Queen of the Day
Having breakfast in bed —
Receives it
With tears in her eyes.

— Gemma Gaye.

Dave grinned.

"Not necessary," he assured her. "I'm a gardener. I assure you my tetanus jabs are right up to date!"

They all sat sipping their tea, while Sophie told them she didn't know what the world was coming to, and what she'd do to the likes of them if she ever got her hands on them. Fancy ganging up on a young lady like that!

Dave smiled at the boy. "Thanks for your help, mate. Proper little terrier this one, Sophie. You should have seen him! As for Melody — well, she could give wildcats lessons!"

'What made you come back?" Melody asked the boy.

"What? Oh, I brought you some flowers from my auntie's garden. You know, to say 'thanks.' But I dropped them. Sorry."

Tears pricked Melody''s eyes. What nice people they were. They'd shown her more warmth and consideration today than Dennis ever had. Why had she ever wasted her time on him?

Memories she'd been trying to keep at the back of her mind began surfacing. She remembered all her hopes and dreams, how betrayed and disillusioned she'd felt when she learned the truth, how she'd lost her faith and self-esteem.

Pain seemed to flood over her, then faded and died. She realised tears were trickling down her cheeks.

"What's wrong, Melody?" Dave asked.

"Nothing, Dave," she told him, smiling weakly. "Absolutely nothing — now!"

It was true. For the first time for many months she felt free and at peace.

Dave looked at her. Huge fingers gently wiped away the tears, and his eyes, now keen and searching, looked into hers. He nodded.

"Whatever it was, the shadows have gone," he agreed.

SHORTLY afterwards they left Sophie's van, promising to call again next Sunday. Melody and Dave took their leave of Percy.

Percy, Melody thought incredulously. He was the most unlikely Percy she could imagine! On second thoughts, maybe he wasn't. He'd certainly been a sort of Scarlet Pimpernel to her, and the Scarlet Pimpernel's name had been Percy Blakeney!

"I'll take you home now," Dave said. "I was going to ask if you'd like a short run into the country, and perhaps a bar meal, before I go to see my sister in hospital, but I really think you've been through enough for one day!"

"I think you could be right," Melody agreed. "I do feel rather tired now."

"Maybe I make a suggestion? Why not come home with me for tea, and then go and see your sister? I hope there's nothing seriously wrong?"

"Oh, it's serious all right. She made me an uncle for the third time yesterday!"

They both laughed.

An Unlikely Cinderella

"Are you sure you don't mind?" he asked anxiously.

"No, Dave, I don't mind at all."

He helped her set the table, and chatted to her whilst she worked in the kitchen. They ate their meal, listened to tapes until it was time for him to leave.

Dave had already cleaned himself up as much as he could. When he picked up his jacket, Melody took it from him.

"You can't go to hospital in that." She held out the Aran jumper. "Try this on," she suggested.

It might have been made to measure.

"At last," she said delightedly. "I was looking for someone it might fit."

"You sound like Prince Charming with the glass slipper!" He laughed.

"Well, I certainly found Cinderella," Melody said with satisfaction.

He protested, "I've been called some things in my time, but Cinderella . . ."

They both laughed.

A T the door, Dave turned. "Thanks for lending me the jumper, Melody.

"You said you'll be coming to help Sylvia at the market again next Sunday. I'll return it to you then — or on Wednesday night, if you'd like to come out for a drink?"

If he'd asked earlier in the day, she'd have refused. Now Melody didn't want to return to her isolated cocoon. It might be safe in there, but it was only existing, not living, and she wanted to live again.

She looked properly at Dave. Without the baggy work clothes, she could see he wasn't stout at all, just big and muscular. His jaw was very firm. His tan came from the outdoors, not from a sunbed or idle hours on a beach.

But she didn't really care about all that. What he was and did was far more important, and he was certainly not another Dennis — he'd already proved that.

She realised he was waiting for her answer. "What time?"

"Eightish?"

"I'll be ready. But don't bring back the sweater, Dave. It's yours now."

He turned to go after he'd thanked her, then paused.

"You haven't forgotten what happened to Cinderella and Prince Charming, have you?" he asked.

"No, Dave, I haven't forgotten. Why?"

"Because I like fairy-tale endings." His eyes teased and were serious at the same time.

Melody watched him out of sight.

Wednesday suddenly seemed much too long to wait for another meeting with her unlikely Cinderella! □

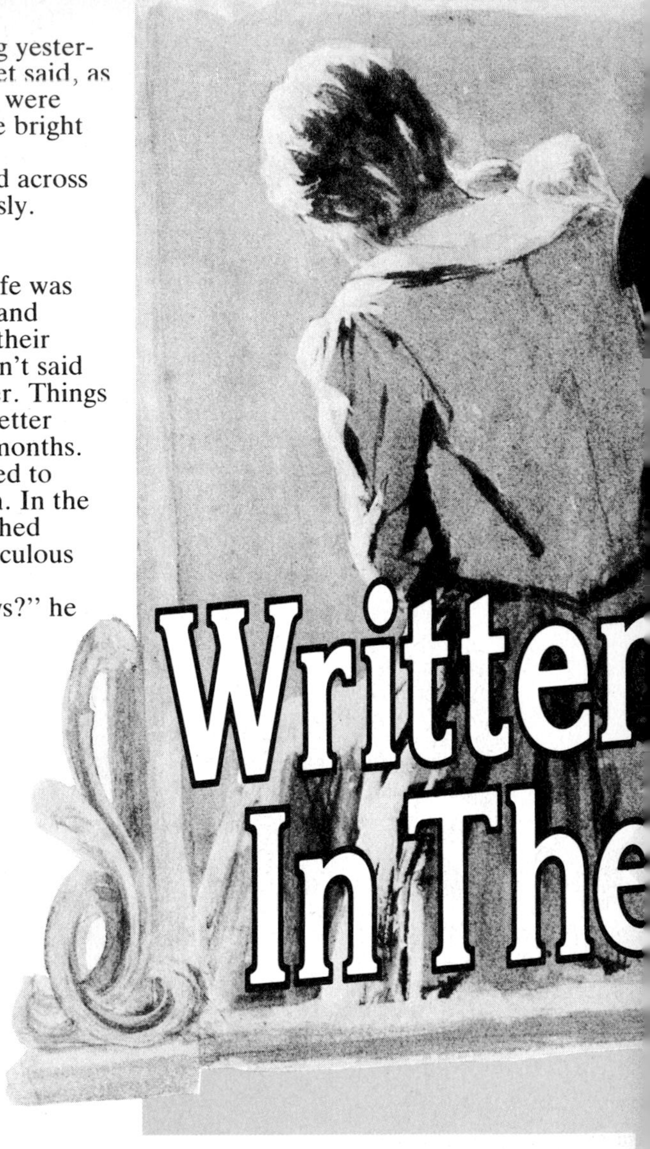

"CHRISTINA rang yesterday," Margaret said, as she and Hugh were having breakfast one bright spring morning.

"Oh?" He glanced across at her rather anxiously. "How are things?"

"I'm not sure."

Hugh knew his wife was trying to stay calm, and prayed silently that their daughter-in-law hadn't said anything to upset her. Things had been so much better during the last few months. They'd even managed to laugh together again. In the old days they'd laughed together at such ridiculous things, but now . . .

"How are the boys?" he inquired, by way of diversion.

"She didn't say."

"Did she want anything in particular?"

"She said she needs to talk. She wants to come over next Saturday, without the boys. Doesn't that strike you as odd? The boys won't be at school on Saturday."

"Not odd really," Hugh began, trying to play down his rising anxiety. "After all, they're not babies any more. It's no longer a treat to come and see Granny and Pop."

MARGARET frowned, pleating the table-cloth with nervous fingers. "Will you be playing golf on Saturday?"

"Unless you'd rather I cancelled it." He pushed away his empty plate, and stood up. "Come on, love, you've got something on your mind."

"I think —" Margaret said, in a carefully controlled voice "— I

156

by GILLY GILES

Stars

think I know why she's not
bringing the boys."

"You do?"

"Can't you guess? It sticks out a mile!
She's met someone to take Richard's place,
and she's coming to tell us about it."

"How can you be so sure?"

"I just know it! I can feel it, here inside me!"

157

Hugh allowed the small silence to deepen before he spoke again. Then he said, "Margaret, dearest, have you forgotten that Christina is still a young, attractive woman? Two school-age boys are no company for her.

"She's lonely. She's been lonely for nearly two years ever since Richard died. You can't expect her to go on grieving for ever. You've got to understand. We both do."

"I do understand!" Her voice was a cry for help. "I do, honestly, Hugh. It's just that it's too soon."

Tears began to pour down her face. "How can I welcome into our home someone who isn't Richard?"

"Don't upset yourself," Hugh pleaded. "Maybe that isn't what she wants to talk about at all. It's only guess-work on your part. Maybe she's worried about the boys. She finds them hard to control without a father to help. Try to relax, at least until we know."

"I'm sorry, Hugh." Her penitence was so genuine. "I shouldn't have flown off the handle like that. Of course Christina has to live her own life, and I *will* accept it, but not just yet."

She blew her nose on a crumpled tissue, and began collecting up the breakfast dishes. "Don't give up your golf for me, darling. You'll see Christina at lunch, and that will be fine. She and I can have a cosy tête-a-tête before you come in. I promise I won't upset her."

"It's all right, love," Hugh said gently. "I understand how you feel, but I don't want you to get ill again. I don't want you re-starting those sleeping pills. You've only just cut them out."

"Dear Hugh, what would I do without you?" Margaret sighed.

"You'd do what Christina has done without Richard," Hugh replied sadly. "You'd square your shoulders and get on with your life."

B Y the time Saturday arrived, Margaret had control of herself, and was busy setting the table when her daughter-in-law arrived, popping in through the open patio doors.

Christina looked fresh and attractive in a crisp dress of multicoloured cotton and carried a bunch of freesias.

"Hi!" she called.

"Goodness! I didn't hear your car."

"I didn't come by car. I got a lift part of the way and walked up from the church," Christina replied.

She pressed the flowers into Margaret's hand. "Your favourites. Oh Margaret, it's good to see you looking so much better. I think the move here has helped.

"It was wonderful walking up the lane. I wish we didn't live in a stuffy old town."

"It is lovely here," Margaret agreed. "Come into the garden. We'll have sherry on the patio."

"Where's Hugh?" Christina asked when they were seated.

"Playing golf as usual, but he'll be home before you go. I think he's being tactful, so that we can have a feminine natter."

As they sipped their sherry in the sunshine, Christina chatted about everything and nothing. Although she looked prettier than ever, Margaret noticed there were shadows beneath her vivid, blue eyes, and there was a certain tenseness about her movements.

Her own gnawing anxiety made her uncomfortable, too, and it seemed the air was fill with nervous expectancy. At last, to bring the conversation round to family, Margaret inquired about her grandsons.

"Phillip's OK," Christina said. "But —" she hesitated "— I'm having problems with Michael."

"Why is it always the elder child who creates problems?" Margaret answered sympathetically. "What exactly are they?"

The colour receded from the younger woman's cheeks, and Margaret held her breath.

"School, mainly," came the reply at last. "He's down from top to nearly bottom of his class, and — and — he's started to play hookey."

"Try not to be too upset. Remember Michael has lost his father. He may still be suffering from reaction."

"I've thought of that, but I don't know what to do."

"Would it be a good idea to have a word with his teacher?" Margaret suggested.

"I've tried that, too," Christina said, "but it hasn't helped."

"Wasn't the teacher sympathetic? What sort of a woman is she? Dose she have children of her own?"

"She's not a woman," Christina said with a faint smile. "She's a man. His name is Rao. He's from Delhi — filling in for a couple of years."

"Oh!" Margaret couldn't hide her surprise. "Not a British teacher? D'you think that could be the trouble?"

"What do you mean?"

Embarrassed, Margaret floundered, "Well, you never know with children."

"Mr Rao is a qualified teacher, admired for his prowess at cricket. A bit hot on discipline, but as far as I know well liked." Christina's voice was non-committal and Margaret glanced at her curiously.

"Then perhaps you should talk to him again. Does he know about Richard?"

Christina nodded, then quite suddenly she crumpled up and put her head in her hands.

"I don't know how to handle it," she sobbed.

"I knew something was worrying you," Margaret said.

She got up and put her arms round the younger woman's shoulders which, she realised, were trembling. "I felt it when you phoned. Come and have some lunch. You'll feel better after a good meal."

A S her daughter-in-law toyed with her food, Margaret tried to keep up a cheery flow of conversation. "Hugh wasn't sure if he'd be in for lunch, but he promised not to miss you.

"Perhaps he could have a talk with young Michael — not a lecture, just a friendly chat. It might help to sort out whatever the trouble is. They've always been pals, haven't they?"

When Hugh breezed in, windswept and hungry, the two women appeared to be relaxing with their coffee. The atmosphere lightened with his uncomplicated presence, and Margaret wallowed in the relief of knowing Christina's news was not what she had feared.

When the time came for the girl to depart, she refused Hugh's offer of a lift to the village.

"I'd rather walk," she explained. "These quiet lanes of yours have a soothing effect on me. You don't know how lucky you are living away from town."

★　　★　　★　　★

"It wasn't what I'd feared after all!" Margaret confessed happily after they'd waved the young widow off. "She's been worrying herself over Michael. I don't know if she's told me everything, but apparently he's been slacking at school, being rude to his teacher and playing hookey. I knew there was something on her mind, but knowing the truth is such a relief."

She picked up her knitting, then laid it down thoughtfully. "Couldn't you have a talk with Michael, Hugh? You could remind him he still has a grandfather. I don't like to think of the lad fretting and no-one understanding the reason."

Hugh looked into her eager face.

"He's probably suffering from unrequited love." He grinned.

"What? At nine years old?"

"Forget it. But I'm glad your mind's easy about the other matter."

Margaret's respite was doomed to be short-lived, for, at that very moment, Christina was ignoring the waiting bus and making for a

SHARING

Health is all the wealth we need,
A richness we can share,
With others not so fortunate,
Who need our love and care.
It's all the efforts that we make,
A sacrifice, a gift,
A contribution, sale of work,
Which can give life a lift,
To those who're suffering every day,
And need a helping hand,
Whose lives depend on folks like us,
Who care and understand.
So as we now attempt to help,
All those who live in pain,
Remember that our efforts can,
Change tears to smiles again.

— *Chrissy Greenslade.*

small sports car parked alongside, its doors flung open ready for her.

"I chickened out!" she cried, tumbling in beside the dark-haired young man behind the wheel. "I couldn't tell them, Anil, I couldn't!

"I'm almost sure Margaret knew, anyway. She was all tensed-up and uneasy, so I just told her about Michael, and you know, she relaxed immediately."

Suddenly she burst into tears.

"Christina! Darling!" His hands covering hers were firm and cool as he listened gravely and impassively with great attention to her story.

When at last he spoke, she thought she'd never heard such tenderness in a man's voice before.

She raised a tearful face to his slow, beautiful smile.

"It's not *all* bad," he whispered. "Something wonderful happened today in school."

"Not Michael?"

"Yes, Michael! He actually came to see me, bearing an olive branch in the shape of a cricket bat."

"He's crazy about cricket."

"He wanted to know if I'd coach him."

"Oh, Anil! I don't know how he dared after —"

"It was his way of apologising. I accepted it unconditionally. So you see, things are moving in the right direction."

"It's wonderful. I can hardly believe it. But I still have to tell the grandparents about — us."

"The time isn't ripe," he said gently. "Not today, but it will be." Then, in a lighter tone he went on, "Next time we'll consult the stars."

"You don't really mean that, or do you?"

"In my country, we always consult the stars before making momentous decisions, and even now, I find it hard to scoff. Would you laugh if I confess to reading our daily horoscopes?"

"I don't know," Christina said. "I suppose I might do. Did you read them today?"

"Certainly I did, while I was sitting in the car waiting for you."

"So what did they foretell?"

"That for you, revelations of the heart were better kept secret until a more propitious date. And for me, better understanding with a young person."

"You're pulling my leg!"

"Only a little bit." Anil's dark eyes were full of mischief. "But the advice is sound in principle. There has to be a right moment for many of our actions, and until it is apparent, we must have patience. Today your courage failed you. Tomorrow, who knows?"

Christina raised her face for his kiss, loving his shining optimism. In his arms she felt warm and safe. Nothing else seemed to matter in this moment of togetherness.

"So we must put our faith in the stars?" she murmured happily.

"We must put our faith in each other," he said. ☐

A LINK IN THE CHAIN

ETHEL put the receiver down and leaned back in her chair thoughtfully. Her caller had been such a nice young woman, and they'd had such a pleasant chat about this and that.

Such a pity that it had turned out to be yet another attempt to sell her something she didn't want and couldn't afford. This time it was double-glazing.

She'd explained very politely that she'd have loved to do the cottage up but, on a widow's pension, it was quite out of the question. Such a pity the young woman had slammed the phone down.

Ethel sighed. Modern manners left a lot to be desired. On the other hand, there was such a thing as being too formal. Her new neighbour was a case in point.

She could see Major Hastings now, out in his garden. He'd mowed the lawn within an inch of its life, and was busy giving the hedge a very business-like short-back-and-sides. In the six months he'd been there, he'd never responded to her gestures of friendship with anything more than a nod and a brisk click of the heels.

She so missed her old, easy-going friends, especially since Harold had passed away. The only company she got was at her weekly visit to the lunch club. The major went there too, but he maintained his polite reserve with everyone.

Yes, Ethel was finding life lonely. That was why she rather welcomed those phone calls, even if they only ever ended with the familiar sales pitch. Still, she supposed, that was

by
CERI EVANS

part of modern life too.

She didn't remember having so many when Harold was alive, although that might have been because he'd usually answered the phone himself, and he'd certainly have given such people short shrift.

She got up to put the kettle on, wondering if she dared invite the major to take a break from his labours. Perhaps not, she thought. It was better not to run the risk of being rebuffed. Besides, it might seem forward . . .

Putting a tray laid for one on the side table, she glanced at the phone, half-expecting it to ring again. Did other people get as many unsolicited calls? Maybe she'd raise the question at tomorrow's club.

THE subject provoked such a furore next day that Ethel almost wished she hadn't mentioned it. Everyone, it seemed, was plagued by them and, to her profound embarrassment, a resolution was passed to write to the local MP. She'd never meant to make trouble, yet she'd inadvertently disturbed a veritable hornet's nest of discontent.

"And what about these door-to-door salesmen?" Mrs Pilkington demanded. "Can't something be done about them? A respectable woman doesn't feel safe in her own home any longer."

Still, one good thing came of it. The major not only stopped to speak to Ethel afterwards, but actually offered to escort her home!

"I trust," he remarked as they reached her gate, "you have a chain on your door."

Ethel shook her head sadly. She could remember the days when village people didn't even shut their doors when they went out, let alone bar them when they were in.

"You should," he said solemnly. "Can't be too careful. Never know who might be on the other side."

Ethel murmured something about getting the local handyman to fit one.

"I'd be only too pleased to do the job for you myself," Major Hastings said with a gallant little bow.

Ethel was pleased to accept — more than pleased, she was delighted, in fact.

It wasn't that she cared about the chain or the bill for fixing it. What was really mattered was that the major had finally broken the ice.

Still, she knew he was right about the chain. She'd been silly not to do something sooner, she reflected that night as she waited for the milk to warm her cocoa, silly to rely on the sense of security Harold's cardigan gave her.

She glanced at it, hanging untouched for nearly a year now on the peg behind the door. The mere suggestion it gave of a man about the place was hardly enough to deter a burglar, after all.

★　　　★　　　★　　　★

The major arrived on the dot of eleven next morning, looking as if he was about to refurbish Fort Knox.

"Might as well do it thoroughly," he muttered. "No point reinforcing the front and leaving the rear unguarded."

Ethel could barely restrain a smile at the way he made putting a couple of bolts on a cottage door sound like a military campaign. But, she had to admit, he did a good job, and tidied up afterwards, too!

She offered him lunch before he set about the chain, but he refused. He had a spot of business in the village.

"Back in about an hour," he said, piling his tools neatly in the corner.

Ethel had just finished washing up when the doorbell rang. Must be Major Hastings being proper again. She couldn't help wishing he'd relax a little and come the back way.

To her surprise, however, she found herself staring not at the lined face with its pale, blue eyes and neat, grey moustache but at the plump and swarthy features of a much younger man.

A Link In The Chain
======

"Good afternoon, madam," he began. "I'm doing a survey . . ."
He glanced over her shoulder and stopped as though entranced by
what he saw.

Ethel followed his gaze and, before she knew what was what, he'd
pushed past her into the hall and, worse, had grabbed a small, china
horse from the hallstand.

Too late, she realised he was yet another of those wretched
"dealers." Usually she managed to shut the door in their faces, but
this one had been too clever for her.

She glanced at the clock. If only the major . . .

"Very fond of these," the man said with an insincere smile. "My
grandmother had one just like it. Got broken, though. Not worth a
lot, but I'd give you a couple of quid for it. For her sake," he added
with a sentimental sigh.

"Hallstand's a bit of a monstrosity," he remarked. "I couldn't offer
you much for it. No call for them nowadays, but I'd take it off your
hands. Probably riddled with woodworm."

Ethel was about to protest when she saw his hand stray towards
her big teapot. She wanted to grab it, clutch it to her protectively.

Yet any sign of panic would give the game away. She breathed
deeply, trying to control herself.

"Hmm," he muttered, examining the object. "I expect you thought
this was solid silver."

"Well . . ."

"Not so. Good imitation, of course. But only plated. This," he said
turning it over, "*looks* like a hallmark. Fake, I can assure you."

He took a jeweller's glass from his pocket and offered it to Ethel.

"I wouldn't know what to look for," she murmured.

He beamed triumphantly. "That's how people like you get caught."

Ethel preserved a dignified silence.

"Give you a tenner for it," he offered. "I'm a fool to myself at that
price."

He strolled into the living-room.

"Now that's more like it." He bent to examine a small, water-
colour landscape on the wall beside the mantelpiece.

"Turn of the century." He nodded. "Very collectable period. This
chap," he added, peering at the signature, "is one of the minor
artists, but he'll be riding on the crest of the others' wave.

"Give you fifty pounds for *that*. No, say sixty. Mind you, I'm
taking a chance. May have to hang on a good while to see that
back."

He paused, fingering the mirror above it. "Seventy for the two.
What d'you say to that?"

I SAY that any business propositions should be addressed to me,"
a man's voice said suddenly, "not to my, er, wife."

Ethel turned and saw the major in the kitchen doorway with a
very severe expression and wearing Harold's cardigan!

165

"I think that's ours," he said, removing the china horse from the dealer's hand before ejecting him over the doorstep.

Ethel watched, relieved. Strange, she thought, how well the cardigan suited the major. Could have been made for him . . .

"I'm sorry about this," he remarked, taking it off once they were alone. "Felt it looked more the part than my sports jacket."

Ethel smiled.

"Hope you didn't think the 'wife' too forward," he went on apologetically.

"Not at all," she murmured. "You had to convince him you meant business."

They were sitting over tea which she poured from the big silver pot.

"I don't often use it," she said, "but this is a special occasion."

"Solid silver, of course," the major noted aloud.

"Oh yes, and old, too. It was one of my great-grandmother's wedding presents, same as the silver mirror."

"That's how the dealers work, you know. Offer you a lot for something worthless and seem to be doing you a favour, then get the valuable stuff for a song."

Ethel nodded. "Shame about the painting, though."

The major looked puzzled. "Don't know much about art."

He cleared his throat in embarrassment.

"I'm afraid it doesn't look like a masterpiece to me," he ventured.

"Oh, it's not. I'd have been delighted with the price he offered me. I've an attic full of the things."

Major Hastings looked slightly crestfallen. "Oh dear, I shouldn't have interfered. After all, rascal though he was, there's no denying he had a point. When a period becomes popular, collectors will pay the earth even for minor artists."

Ethel burst into laughter. "Period! Minor artist! Oh Major, fond as I was of my husband, I can't pretend he was anything but the very worst amateur when it came to painting! I've only kept that one on the wall for sentimental reasons."

THERE," the major said, standing back and surveying his handiwork with satisfaction. "That should put paid to any more intruders. It would take a rogue elephant to break that chain."

Ethel smiled. "It looks magnificent."

There was a slight pause, then the major coughed awkwardly. "Perhaps I might be permitted to call on you one day, purely to check that you're managing to use it."

"Any time," Ethel murmured. "You're welcome to call at any time."

Very welcome, she repeated to herself as she hung Harold's cardigan carefully back in its place. It hardly seemed worth putting it away — not when there was the faintest suspicion in the back of her mind that it might well get worn again in the not too-distant future! □

The Wrong Impression

by GRACE MACAULAY

JUNE KINKAID looked at her watch and then bit consideringly on her lower lip while she studied the blouse and skirt on the model in the shop window.

She was only supposed to take an hour off for lunch. She would be late now if she went into the shop, but she felt instinctively that this was the outfit she had been searching for. The combination of shades of green and purple seemed utterly irresistible.

Ten minutes later the clothes were hers, and as she hurried back to work, she told herself, "You're supposed to get this thrill about antiques, June, not new clothes. The truth is, your heart isn't truly in antiques."

There was no space to do more than hang the carrier bag on the hook on the back of the door in the tiny room which she occupied in the firm of Macneil and Grant, Auctioneers, Valuators and Antique Dealers. She would have loved to take out the new garments and admire them again.

It was just as well she didn't because there was a tap on the door and Forbes Macneil, the senior partner, spoke in his slow, pedantic way.

"We've decided to send you out on a call this afternoon, Miss Kinkaid. One of our clients wishes to dispose of an item of value. If you'll come into my office, I'll provide you with full details."

June was amazed at her own eagerness to follow Mr Macneil and to listen to his instructions, as he gave her the cash she would require for the transaction.

She had been with the firm for six months now, and this was only the third time she had been sent out alone — and in the company car, too!

It was wonderful to feel responsible and trusted. She knew that the partners considered her to be very young, but although she was only 22, June had accumulated a wealth of experience because she had been in the business virtually all her life.

Her earliest memories were all of watching and listening to her father, who was an auctioneer. When she decided to make her career in the business, her father had advised her, "You must get some quality training away from home before I'd be willing to take you on as a partner."

Time had flown by at first while she spent a year in Birmingham, then a year in London with reputable firms, but her agreed year in this small, midlands town was beginning to drag.

She felt that she had served her apprenticeship and she was impatient to move on.

NOW as she drove out to the sedate surburbs, June was aware of a familiar knot of excitement tightening her stomach muscles. She wondered what the client wanted to sell.

"Mrs Redford?" June smiled at the elderly woman and said, "I'm June Kinkaid, from Macneil and Grant's. You're expecting me to call, I believe?"

As she spoke, she gave Mrs Redford her business card.

"Yes, come away in, Miss Kinkaid." Mrs Redford returned her smile, but as she led the way to her large, sunny kitchen at the back of the house, she said rather sharply, "You understand, I suppose, that this matter is completely confidential."

"Certainly, Mrs Redford," June replied. "You can rely on our discretion."

"Good! We'll start with a nice cup of tea." Mrs Redford indicated a chair at the table where dainty cups and saucers were set out waiting.

No sooner was the tea poured than there was the sound of footsteps on the gravel and the old woman gave a guilty start. "Oh dear, that must be my grandson — I always know his step."

"That's all right," June said quickly. "I can come back later."

The man who came in was tall and blond. June's eyes met his with a strange feeling of recognition, although she had never seen him before.

Mrs Redford performed the introductions with a hint of agitation, but she told June quite proudly, "Andrew is a doctor at the hospital."

Then, smiling up at him, she asked, "Will you fetch another cup for yourself, Andrew?"

Andrew nodded. "Sure, Grandma."

But he had spotted the engraved business card which June had given to his grandmother, and his mouth tightened ominously.

June Kinkaid was already on her feet, saying casually, "Nice to meet you, Doctor Redford, but I'm afraid it's time — " She halted, experiencing a sense of shock as she encountered his icy glare.

" — Time you were leaving, Miss Kinkaid," Andrew Redford retorted coldly. Opening the back door, he told his grandmother, "I'll just escort Miss Kincaid to her car."

June managed to give the old woman a smile as she said, "Thank you for the tea, Mrs Redford. I'll see you soon."

As she went outside, she told Andrew Redford, "I can find my own way — "

"I've no doubt," he cut in, "but I prefer to see your type safely off the premises."

"I beg your pardon?" June looked at him in astonishment.

"Please — don't bother with your charming innocence act. I saw your visiting card on the table." Andrew ground out the words as he tried to contain his anger.

THEY were walking down the drive by now, and June turned to face him. "There's some mistake here."

Then she paused and clamped her mouth shut. Her loyalty to her client was more important than what this man thought.

She tilted her chin higher and continued towards her car without saying more.

Andrew Redford was not totally immune to the look of appeal she gave him, but his grandmother's welfare was his concern.

He felt obliged to speak to the girl with extreme severity as she unlocked her car. "I advise you not to attempt to return to this house, Miss Kinkaid! My grandmother is very old, and although you took advantage of the fact that she was alone this afternoon, I can assure you that seldom happens. She is a much-loved and well-protected lady."

Then as the girl got into the car, he kept the door open and told her, "Now that I know you're working in this district, I'll warn the family and the neighbours to be on the look-out for you."

He closed the car door, and she drove away without looking at him again. Her face was bright scarlet and he thought, at least she has the decency to blush. Had he imagined the glint of tears in her eyes?

He returned to the house feeling sad somehow, now that his anger had evaporated. He noticed that the card was gone from the table.

His grandmother had an air of evasiveness as she said, "Isn't that Miss Kinkaid a pretty girl?"

"Yes, Grandma," Andrew replied, "but I'm not so easily taken in by a pretty face. And you shouldn't be either!

"Don't you realise that it was unwise to let her into your house? Don't you know that these antique dealers prey on elderly people?"

"Andrew! What did you say to that young woman?" Mrs Redford stared at him in horror.

"I sent her away with a flea in her ear," Andrew answered. "She won't bother you again."

"Oh dear!" Mrs Redford took the card out of her pocket, and said, "I didn't realise you had seen this."

She sighed deeply and shook her head. "I'm getting too old for secrecy and intrigue."

Andrew gazed at her anxiously. She seemed pale and confused, but when he touched her wrist, she snatched her hand away. "Just you leave my pulse alone! No wonder I'm all upset! Macneil and Grant are reputable people. I've dealt with them in the past and I've never felt cheated.

"Naturally they were the people I rang this morning when . . ."

She stopped and pursed her lips. She had no intention of telling him any more.

▶ *over*

RYE, SUSSEX

Set in the Romney Marshes, Rye was a fortified seaport in mediaeval times, but today the town is two miles from the sea. It was one of the original Cinque Ports, and was a target for attack by French raiders from the sea. Today it's a popular spot for holidaymakers. The Romney Marshes as a whole are an attractive area, and become especially atmospheric when sea mists creep in to re-create the days when smuggling abounded.

RYE, SUSSEX : J CAMPBELL KERR

Andrew was aghast as he thought of the lovely girl to whom he had spoken so unjustly.

He asked the old lady, "Do you mean to tell me that you intended to sell something?"

When she remained silent, he said softly, "The cat's well out of the bag now, Gran, so you may as well be straight with me. Did you get a big bill in the post this morning? Something you think you can't pay?"

After a while, she indicated the blank screen on her television set. "That machine gave a great bang last night. I had to go to bed without even seeing the news.." She added, "The engineer said this morning that it's beyond repair."

Andrew was perplexed. "But my father looks after your affairs. Why didn't you phone him? You can easily afford a new television.

"What about all that money your cousin left you in her will last year?"

Mrs Redford frowned. She had forgotten about that. This morning it had seemed like an emergency which made her climb upstairs for the first time in years. She had felt quite triumphant when she took the necklace out of her pocket to admire it!

Andrew thought she had fallen asleep. He stretched his hand out to lift the card which was again lying on the table.

At once, his grandmother began to explain. "I was in a panic, Andrew. I miss my television dreadfully already! I enjoy watching it so much.

"I often wish my own grandmother had had one. She used to sit just staring into the fire and twiddling her thumbs."

Andrew stood up and came round to give her a kiss and a hug.

"Darling Grandma, you won't have to do that," he promised her. "I'll go right now and fetch my portable TV to lend you until we get you a nice new one. OK?"

She nodded and patted his hand gratefully. She felt quite tired out with all the turmoil of the day.

Andrew felt a renewed sense of guilt as he drove towards the hospital to collect his portable from his room. He must ring up and apologise, he told himself, recalling the attractive blush on June Kinkaid's face as she drove away from his unwarranted abuse.

She'll hang up if I phone her, he thought.

Then he saw a florist's shop ahead, and hope seemed to soar in his heart as he started to brake.

JUNE had driven aimlessly around the town for a while. She felt thoroughly humiliated and shattered by her experience.

She headed back to the showrooms, thinking that at least she would not have to face either of the partners until tomorrow.

If one of them had been available, I wouldn't have been sent out, she reminded herself. Obviously, they realise that I must be unsuitable for the job. I look too much like a crook, she told herself despondently.

Inside her office, she closed the door and sat down at her desk, Two forlorn tears slid down her cheeks.

She rubbed them away and looked at the telephone. A little sympathy and understanding from her father might help. But no, she would wait until this evening to phone him, when there would be no-one around to see her wallowing in tears.

She was sitting glumly with her chin in her hands, when the door opened to admit an enormous bouquet of pink roses carried by the showroom assistant.

"These have just been delivered for you, Miss Kinkaid!"

June took the flowers in amazement. Then she opened the envelope to read the card on which Andrew Redford had written on both sides.

Please accept these flowers as a sincere token of my apologies. May I take you out to dinner and apologise in person? I'll phone you to confirm.

June's eyes flew to the bag with her new clothes. Fate must have enticed me to buy that outfit, she decided.

★   ★   ★   ★

Over dinner that evening, Andrew said to her, "Sorry seems such an inadequate word to express what I mean, June. I can hardly believe that you've forgiven me."

He gave her a smile which made her pulses flutter.

"Let's agree to forget that misunderstanding," June said, returning his smile.

"And start all over again?" he suggested. "From the moment we first set eyes on each other?"

"At your grandmother's house." June nodded, recalling the recognition she had sensed.

"She's a special lady, your grandmother," she added softly.

Andrew raised his glass. "Here's to another very special lady."

June blushed.

And as their wine glasses tilted and touched, the sparkling wine lent a shimmering promise to the atmosphere . . . □

Printed and published in Great Britain by D. C. Thomson & Co., Ltd., Dundee, Glasgow and London. © D.C. Thomson & Co., Ltd., 1992. While every reasonable care will be taken, neither D. C. Thomson & Co., Ltd. nor its agents will accept liability for loss or damage to colour transparencies or any other material submitted to this publication.

ISBN 0-85116 549-4